Violin
92VN

Doris Gazda & Albert Stoutamire

Spotlight on Strings

D1486819

Level 1

TECHNIQUE AND PROGRAM MUSIC FOR STRING ORCHESTRA AND INDIVIDUAL INSTRUCTION

CONTENTS

Spotlight on Strings, Level 1 is available for Violin, Viola, Cello, String Bass, Teacher Score/Keyboard.

ISBN 0-8497-3341-3

INTRODUCTION

Welcome to the world of strings! Playing the violin is very exciting. With a violin in your hands, this book on your stand, and a teacher by your side, you have a wonderful chance to become an accomplished string player.

In order for you to be successful, you must:

1. Try as hard as you can to do everything correctly.
2. Find a time and place to practice regularly at home.
3. Ask your family to listen to you play your pieces.
4. Remember to bring your instrument and music to school on your lesson day. Have a pencil with you, too.

Before starting to play, you have several important tasks:

LEARN TO TAKE CARE OF YOUR VIOLIN

1. Keep it in the case when you are not playing it. Make sure your case is completely closed and latched before picking it up.
2. Clean it with a soft cloth before you put it away.
3. Store it where it will not get too hot or too cold.
4. Ask your teacher to check the bridge and tune the strings. Do not try to adjust it or repair it yourself.

LEARN TO TAKE CARE OF YOUR BOW

1. Each time you play your violin, tighten your bow so that a pencil will just barely slide between the hair and the stick.
2. Rosin the bow about 10 times back and forth before you play.
3. Wipe off the stick and loosen the hair before you put the bow back into the case.
4. Do not touch the hair at any time.

BE ABLE TO IDENTIFY AND NAME THE PARTS OF YOUR VIOLIN AND BOW

When you **PRACTICE** at home, remember to:

1. Stand up and play in front of a mirror.
2. Hold your violin and bow correctly.
3. Play for your family.
4. Take care of your violin and bow.
5. Put them in your case carefully and store your case away from excessive heat or cold.

THE VIOLIN AND THE BOW - NAMES OF PARTS

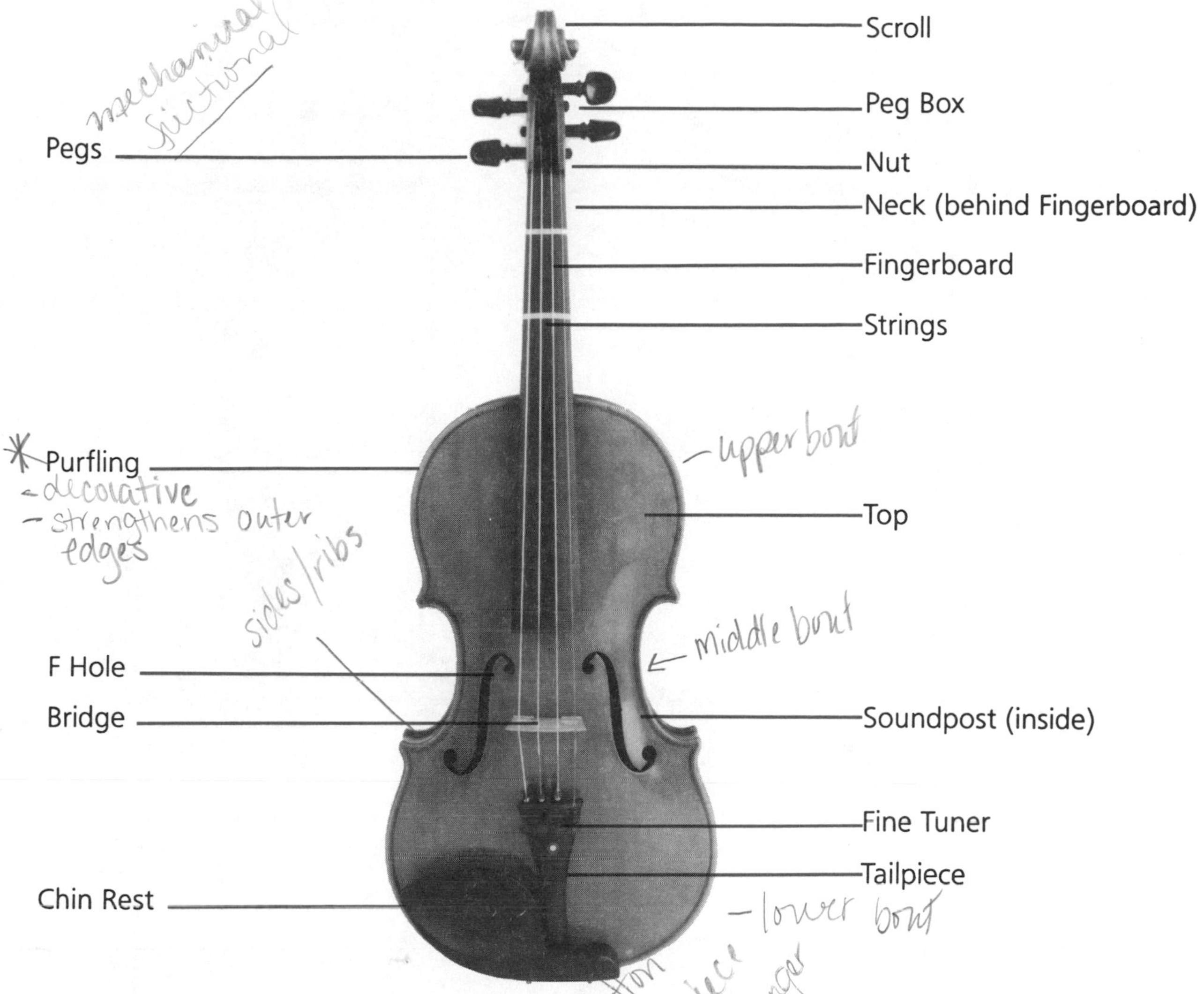

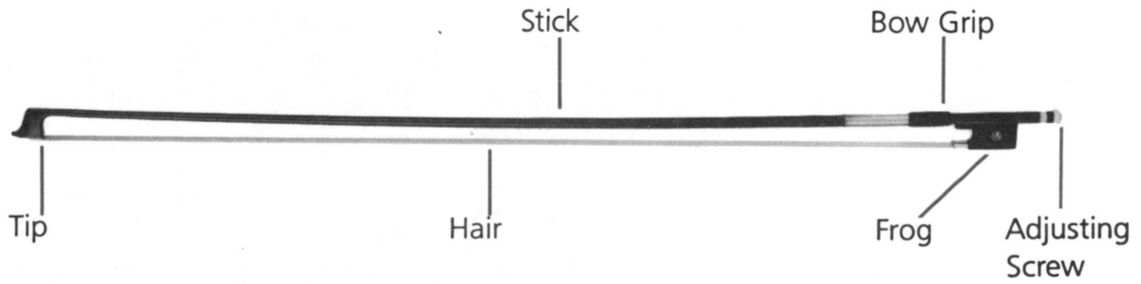

I Open Strings Pizzicato

Playing Pizzicato

Open String Names

G D A E

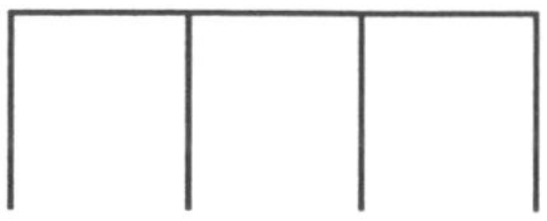

Pizzicato or pizz. - Pluck the strings. Place your right thumb on the corner of the fingerboard and pluck the strings with your first finger over the fingerboard.

Beats - Steady pulses felt or heard in music like ticks of a clock.

Holding Your Violin

PREPARATION POSITION

PLAYING POSITION

Exercises

1. Pluck the strings four times each while keeping time with a steady beat:

G G G G / D D D D / A A A A / E E E E

2. Pluck the strings in reverse order given above.

Improvising Music

1. Say your name aloud. Pluck your open strings so that the tones sound like your name. Think of other names or places and pluck tones that sound like them.
2. Tell a story and pluck your strings for sound effects like background music in a movie or on TV. This is called **IMPROVISING.**

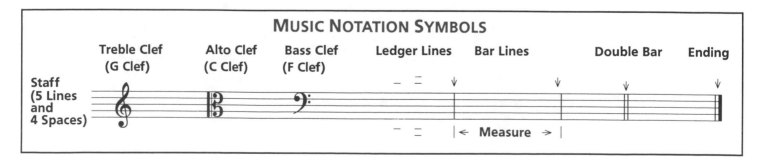

Music Notation Symbols

Treble Clef (G Clef) **Alto Clef (C Clef)** **Bass Clef (F Clef)** **Ledger Lines** **Bar Lines** **Double Bar** **Ending**

Staff (5 Lines and 4 Spaces)

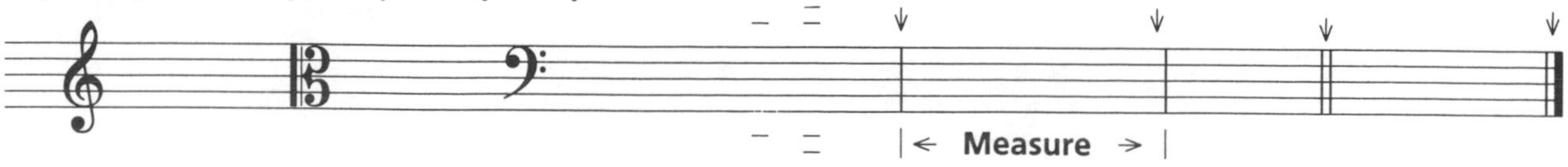

Reading Music and Playing Pizzicato

Open Strings Notation

Quarter Note ♩ or ♩ — one beat of sound

Quarter Rest — one beat of silence

Time Signature

4/4 (4) four beats in a measure
(4) a quarter note or quarter rest receives one beat

1. Rhythm Study *Play on each string.* Change right arm levels when you change strings.

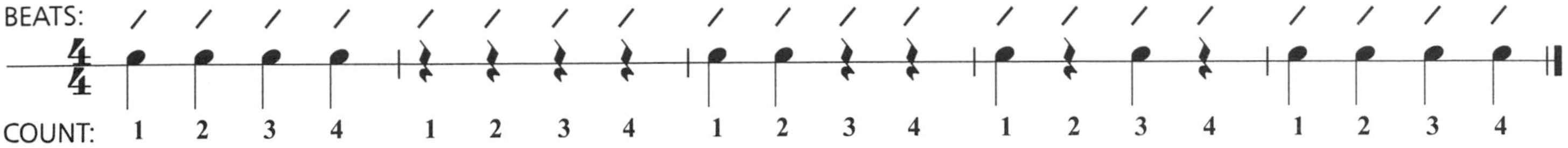

Writing Music

Turn to page 34, line #1. Follow the directions.

2. Four Notes or Rests in a Measure

3. Strum! Strum! Strum! Take your right hand thumb off of the fingerboard and pluck GIANT CIRCLES across all strings with your right hand first finger. Strum from the lowest to the highest string.

4. Note, Note, Note, Rest

5. Two by Two

Writing Music

Turn to page 34, line #2. Follow the directions.

6. Marching Along Together

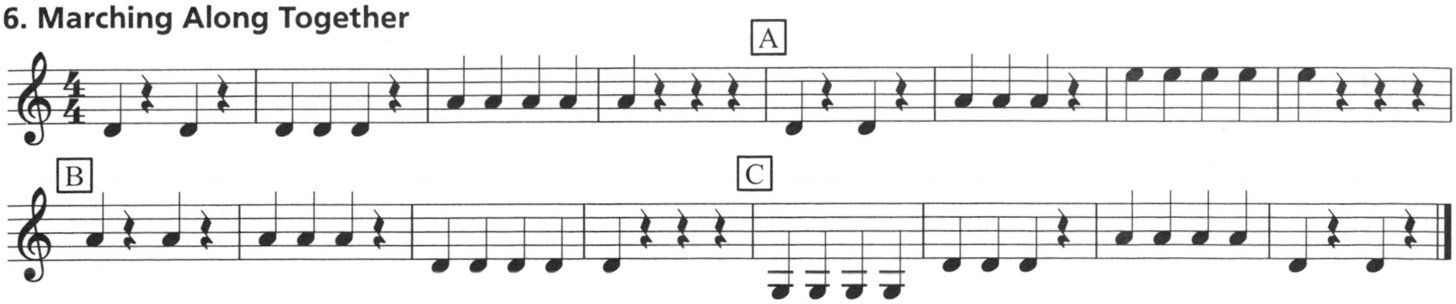

After you learn how to use the bow, play each song on this page (except #3) with the bow.

II Open Strings Arco

THUMB MEETS THE SECOND FINGER

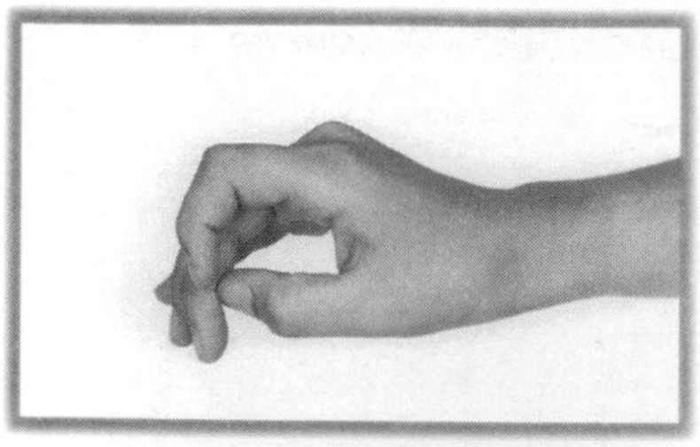

BOW HAND - Front

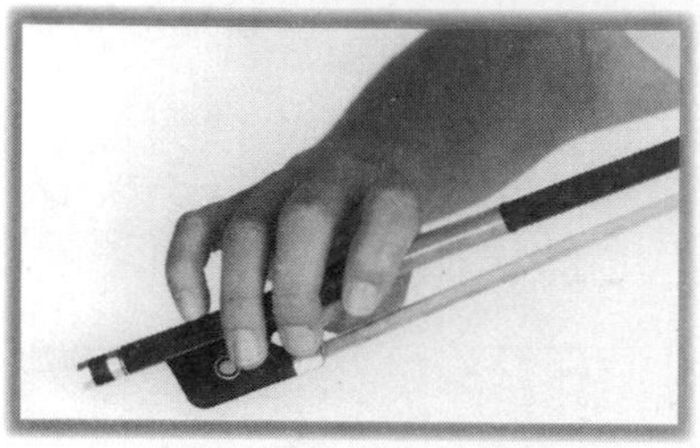

BOW HAND - Back

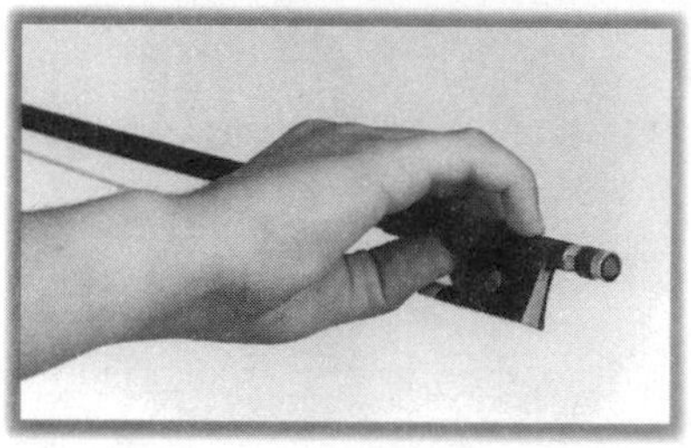

Check your bow hand position with the pictures.

BOWING POSITION

Bowing Exercises

A. Holding the Bow

1. **PLAYING ON THE ROSIN:** Hold the bow in correct position with the right hand. Place the hair on a cake of rosin held in the left hand. Draw the bow back and forth.

2. **THROUGH THE TUNNEL:** While holding the bow in correct position with the right hand, hold the tip of the bow in the left hand. Move the bow back and forth at waist level parallel to the floor as if taking it through a tunnel.

3. **FLYING:** Hold the tip of the bow with the left hand and hold the frog with the right hand in correct playing position. Wave both hands up and down like the wings of a bird.

4. **ROCKET:** Hold the bow in correct position with the right hand. Hold the bow with tip end straight up. Move the bow straight up and down.

5. **WINDSHIELD WIPER:** While holding the bow with the correct right hand position, rotate the arm to make the bow describe an arc.

B. Drawing the bow on the open strings of the violin

SPECIAL NOTE: *Be sure to change bow arm levels when you change strings.*

1. Draw the bow back and forth eight times on each string.
2. Draw the bow on two strings at a time.
3. Make up rhythms using word phrases to play on open strings. (for example: "Mis-sis-sip-pi Mud")

Improvising Music

Find a partner to "talk to" by improvising a phrase (musical sentence) on an open string. Your partner can answer by playing a phrase back to you. Try to tell each other a short story. Then change partners.

C. **PUMP HANDLE** - a silent exercise. Hold the bow at the frog with the correct hand position. Rest the hair on the strings. Move the entire arm up and down in an arc so that the bow swings to the level of each string.

D. Return to page 5 and play the exercises and melodies with the bow.

Reading Music and Playing Arco

Whole Note	**Whole Rest**	**Eighth Notes**
four beats of sound	four beats of silence	one beat of sound

Bowing Symbols

Arco
Draw the bow on the strings.

⊓ Down Bow
Draw the bow across the strings from frog to tip.

V Up Bow
Draw the bow across the strings from tip to frog.

, Lift Bow
Lift the bow off the string and replace it toward the frog.

1. Rhythm Study

Play on each string. Change bow arm levels when you change strings.

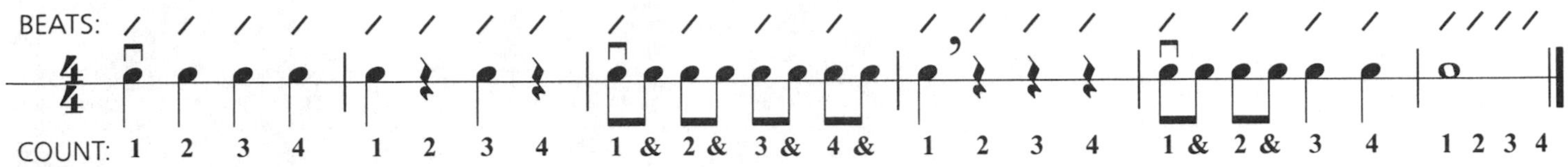

2. Eighth Notes

* Prepare your arm for the next string.

3. Quarters and Eighths

Turn to page 34, line #3. Follow the directions.

4. Fiddle Faddle Bam Bam

5. Marching Along Again

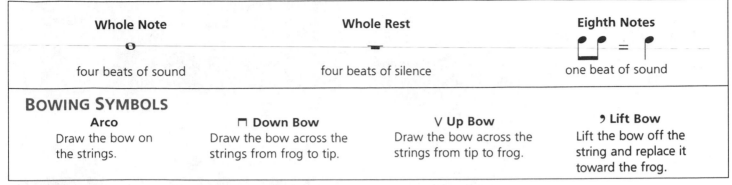

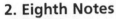

Half of the class may play "Marching Along Again" arco while the other half plays "Marching Along Together" (p. 5) pizzicato.

This page may also be played pizzicato.

III *Left Hand Fingering*

The Major Fingering Pattern

FINGERING	FINGERING PLACEMENT	ILLUSTRATION
0	All fingers above the strings.	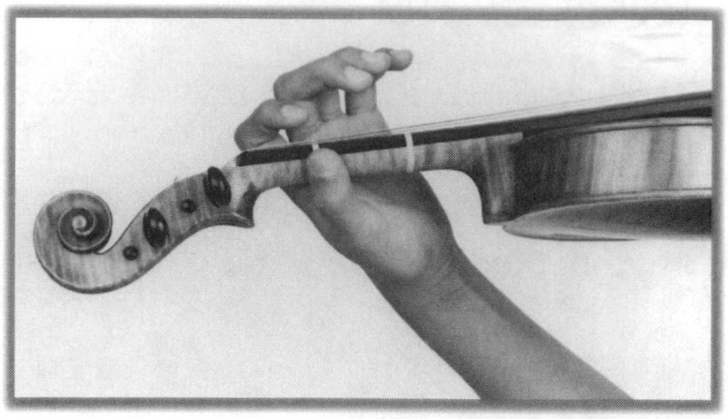
1	First finger down on a string.	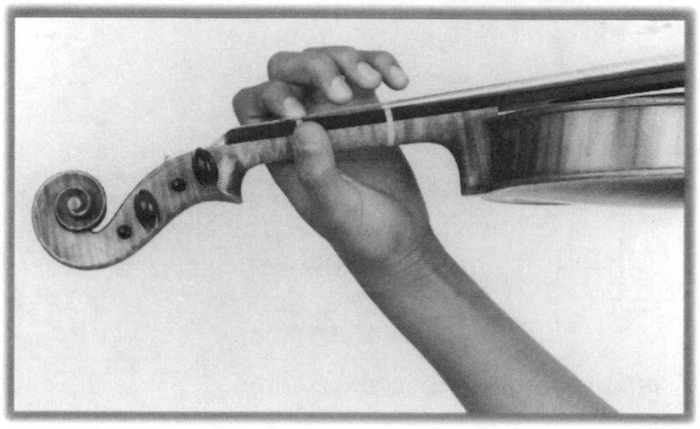
2	Two fingers down on a string.	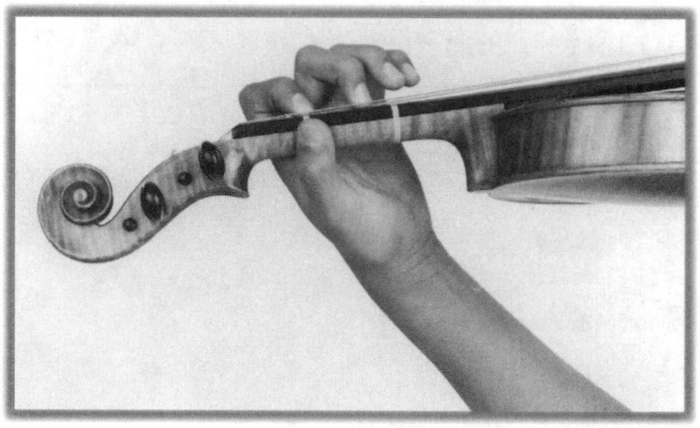
3	Three fingers down on a string.	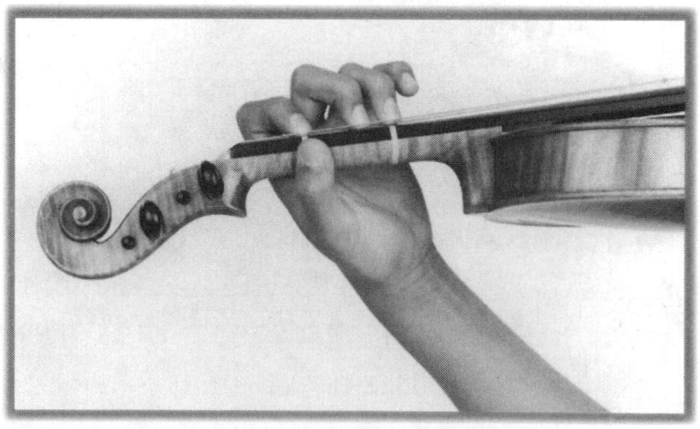
4	Four fingers down on a string.	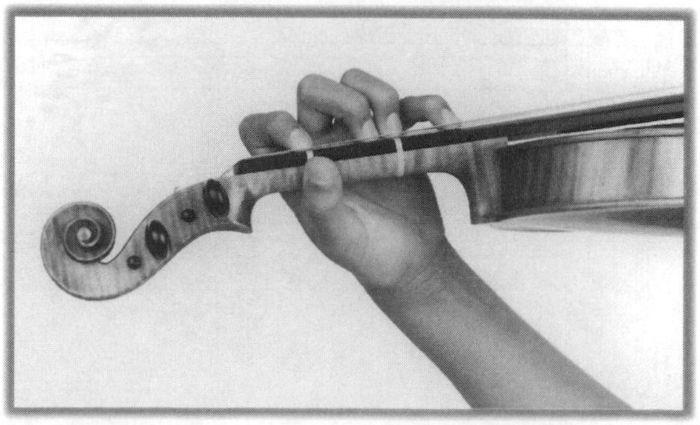

Playing the Major Fingering Pattern

Play each rhythm and fingering study pizzicato and then arco on each string.
Violin and Bass: G, D, A, E   Viola and Cello: G, D, A, C

1. Four Finger Count Down

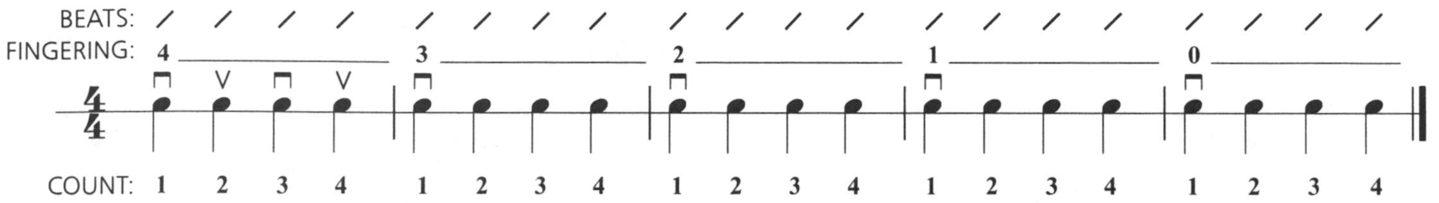

2. Super, Dooper Sky Ride

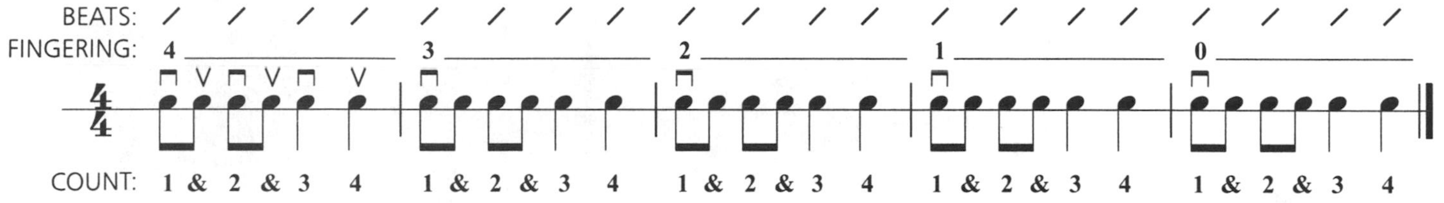

3. Open Up!

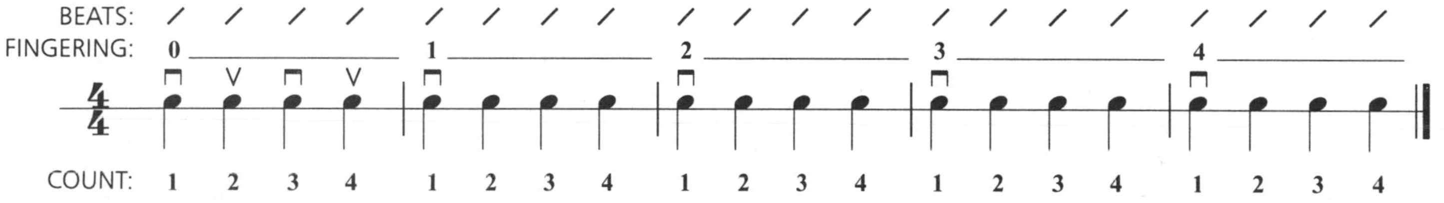

4. Down Diddle, Up Diddle

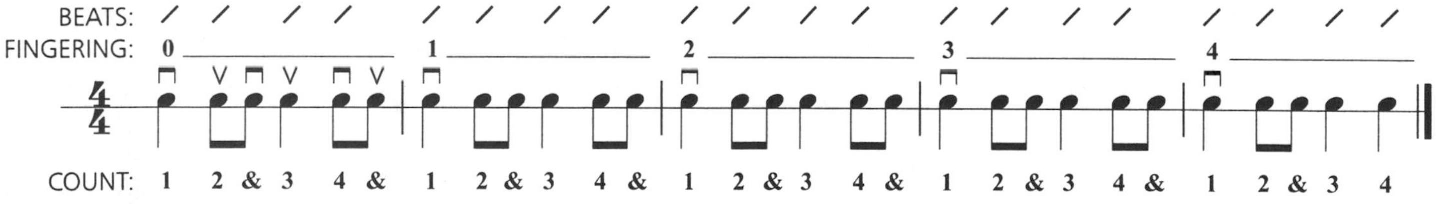

Improvising Music

Improvise a short rhythm on one open string. Next, try playing your rhythm arco or pizzicato with each left hand finger down. Teach it to your class.

5. The Wave

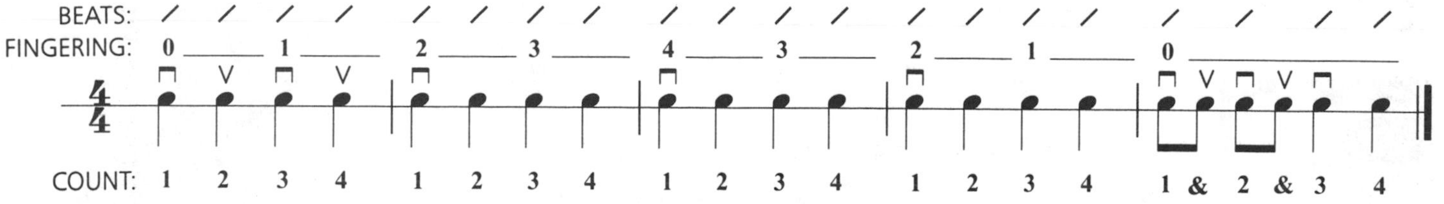

IV Open and One Whole Step

Open - One: The First Two Notes of the Major Fingering Pattern

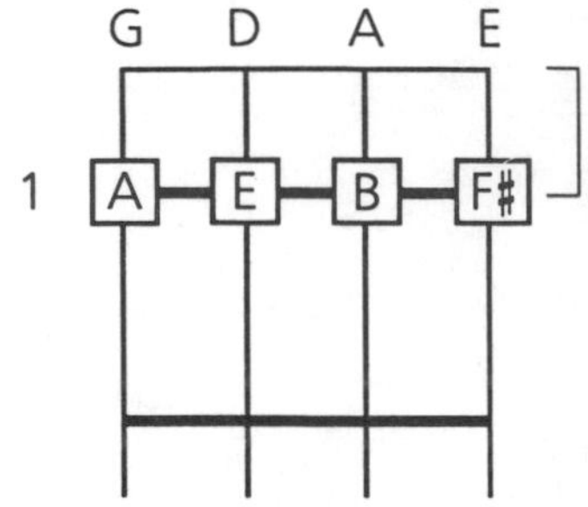

♯ Sharp

A *sharp* is a sign that raises the pitch of a note a half step. The sharp sign next to the F changes the F to an F♯.

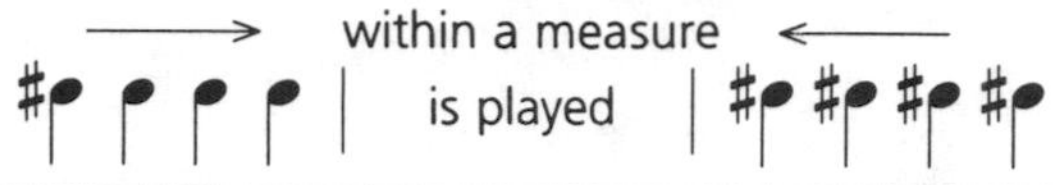

G String

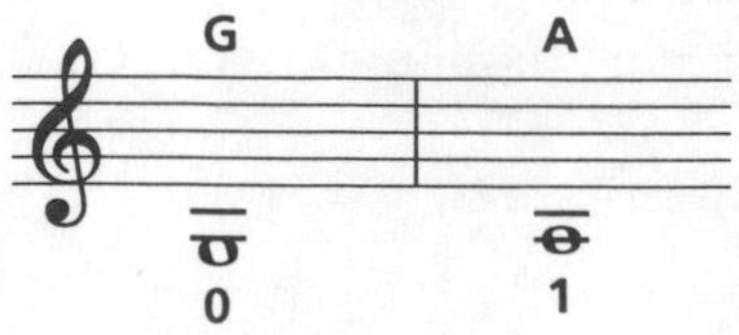

D String

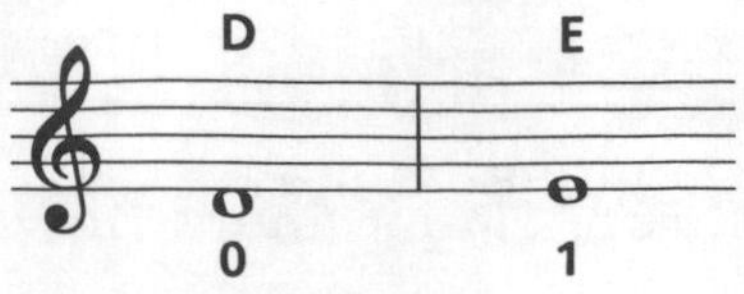

A String

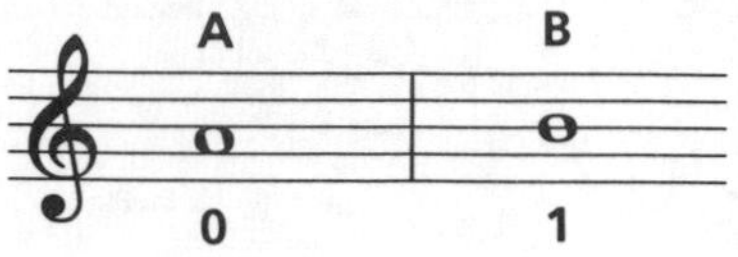

E String

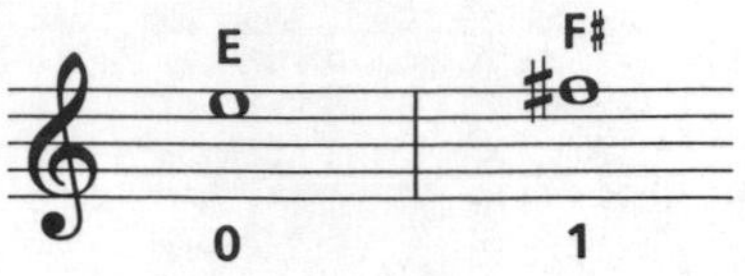

Intervals

An **interval** is the distance in pitch between two tones.

The distance between an open string and the first finger down is a **whole step**.

A whole step is also called an *interval* of a **major second**.

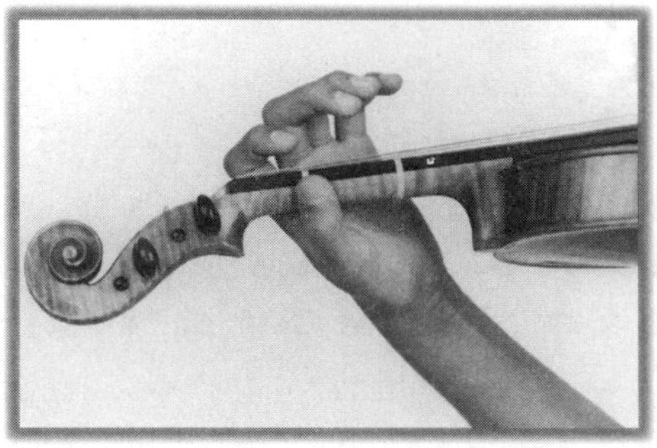

OPEN

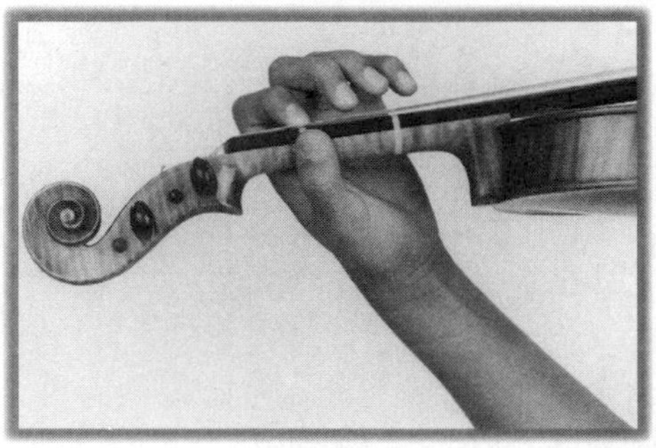

FIRST FINGER DOWN

1. First Finger on the G String

2. First Finger on the D String

3. First Finger on the A String

4. First Finger on the E String

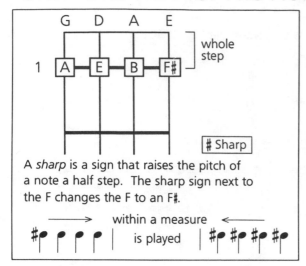

E String: violin and bass only
C String: viola and cello only

Writing Music

Turn to page 34, line #4. Follow the directions.

Melodies Using Open and One

Half Note	**Half Rest**
𝅗𝅥 or 𝅗𝅥	𝄼
two beats of sound	two beats of silence

1. Rhythm Study *Play on each string.*

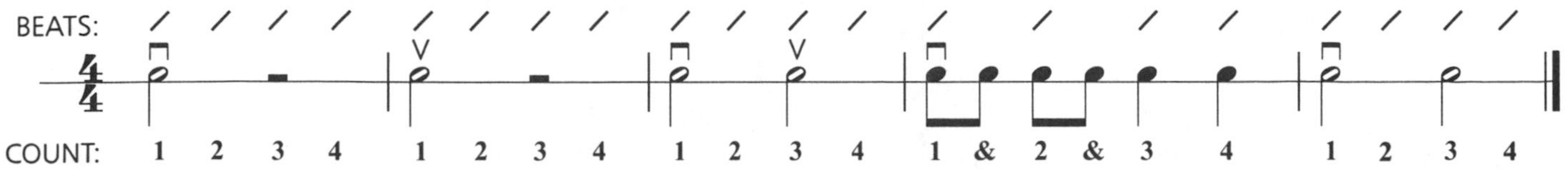

2. Half Note Study

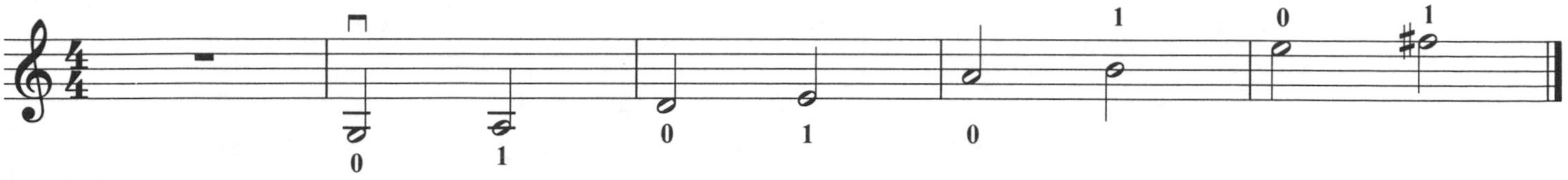

3. Meditation

4. Locomotive, Locomotive Choo-Choo

5. Turning Cartwheels, Head Over Heels

1. Improvise a melody with long, slow tones using open strings and the first finger.
2. Improvise a melody with fast sounds using only the open strings.

6. Open-One Blues

V Open and Two Whole Steps

The First Three Notes of the Major Fingering Pattern

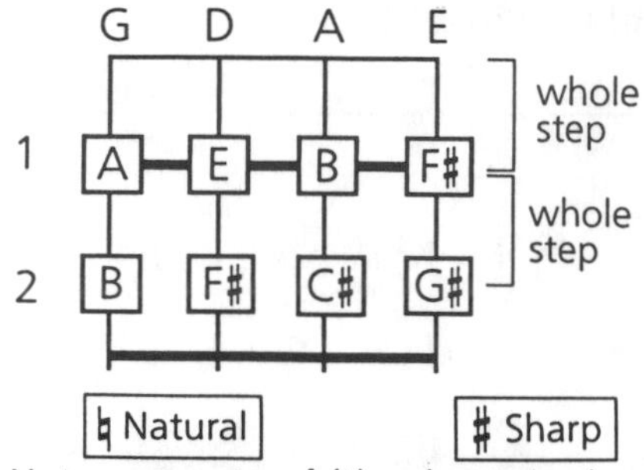

Notes are **natural** (♮) unless raised or lowered by an accidental. When a **sharp** (♯) is an accidental, it raises a tone a half step.

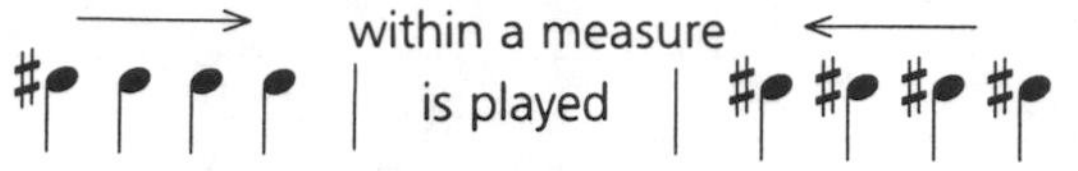

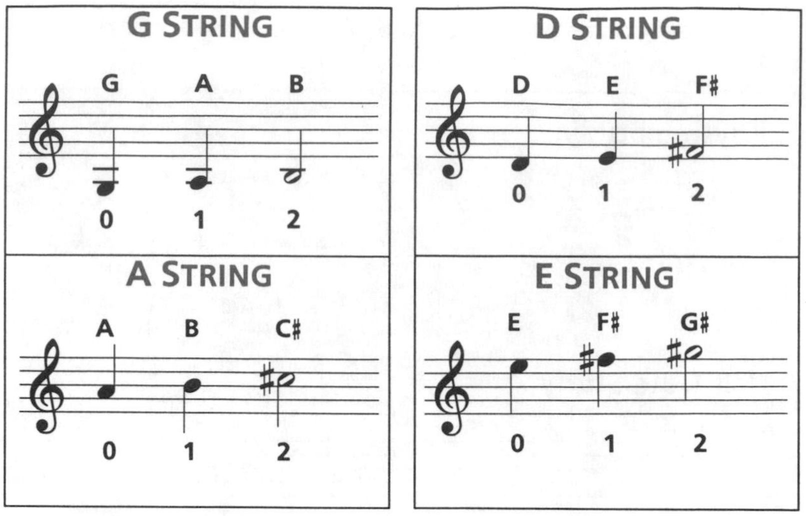

In the major fingering pattern, the distance between the first finger down and the second finger down is a **whole step**.

The distance between the open string and two fingers down is two whole steps.

Two whole steps are called the *interval* of a **major third**.

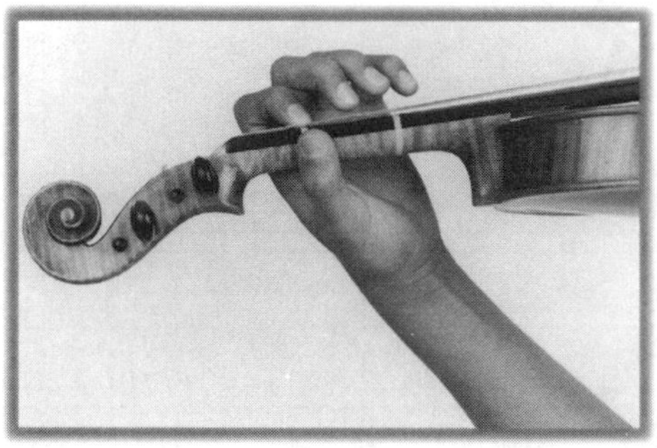

FIRST FINGER DOWN

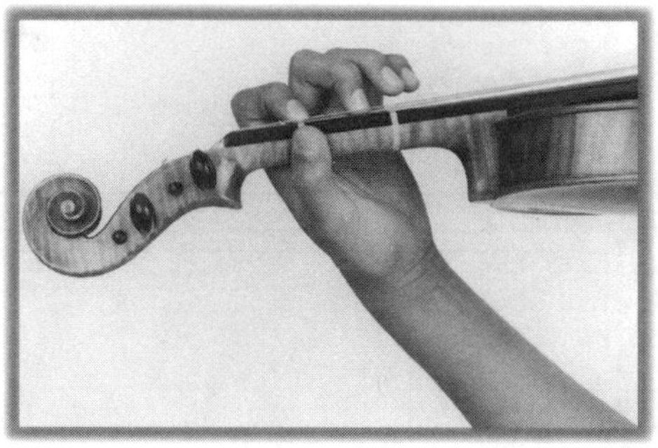

TWO FINGERS DOWN

1. Whole Steps on the G String

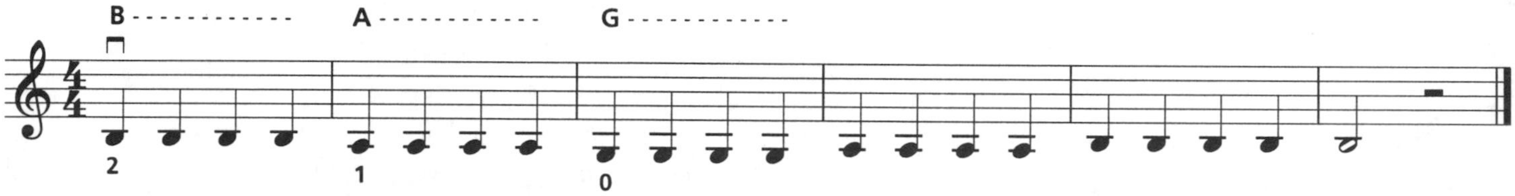

2. Whole Steps on the D String

3. Whole Steps on the A String

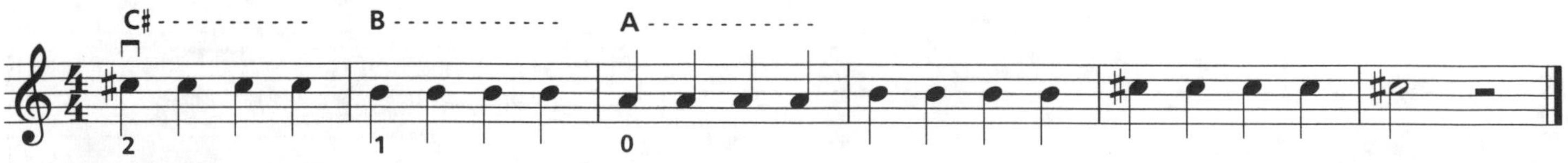

Writing Music

Turn to page 34, line #5. Follow the directions.

4. Whole Steps on the E String

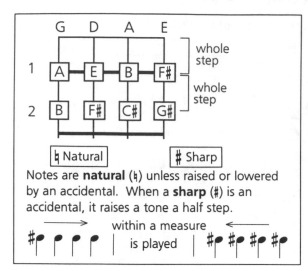

E String: Violin and Bass only
C String: Viola and Cello only

Melodies Using the First Three Notes of the Major Fingering Pattern

Repeat Signs

Go back to the beginning and play again. Play the music between these signs again.

1. Hot Cross Buns English Folk Song

E String: Violin and Bass only. *C String: Viola and Cello only.*

2. Mary's Lamb Traditional

Play *Mary's Lamb* as written.
Then improvise:

1. Change each ♩ (quarter note) to ♫ (two eighth notes).
2. Change the F♯s to open A or open D, or any other note.

Remember that your improvised piece should still sound something like *Mary's Lamb*.

3. Go Tell Aunt Rhody Traditional

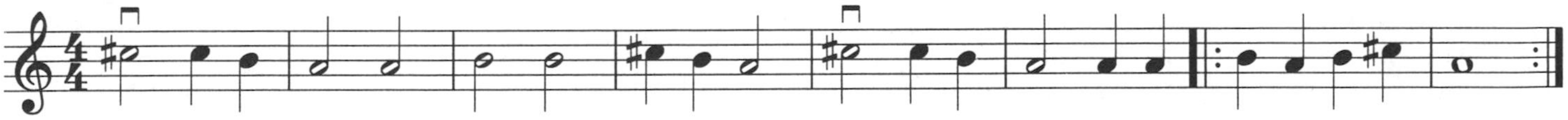

4. Au Claire de la Lune French Folk Song

5. Jolly Old St. Nick Traditional American Song

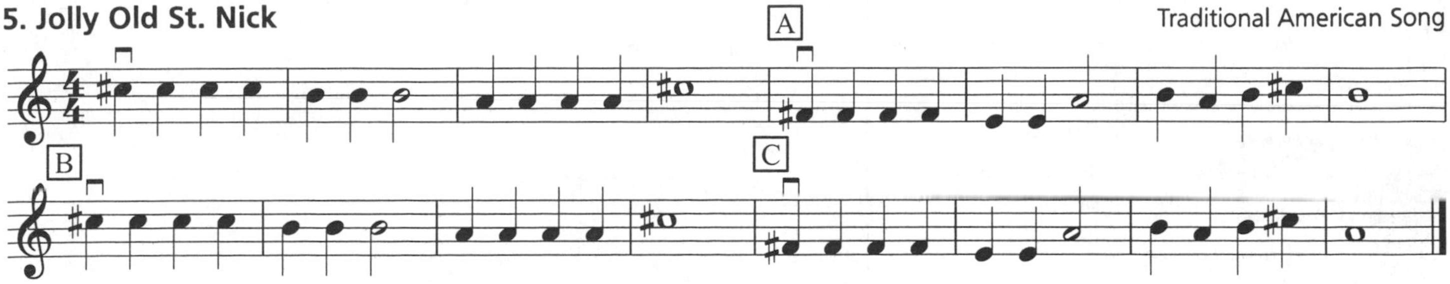

VI Four Note Major Fingering Pattern

Two Whole Steps and a Half Step

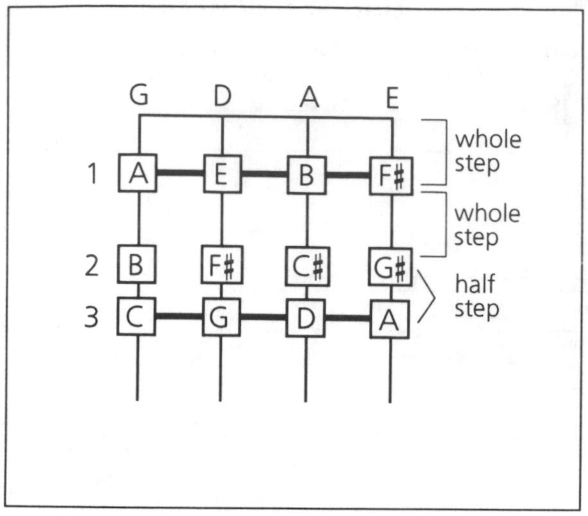

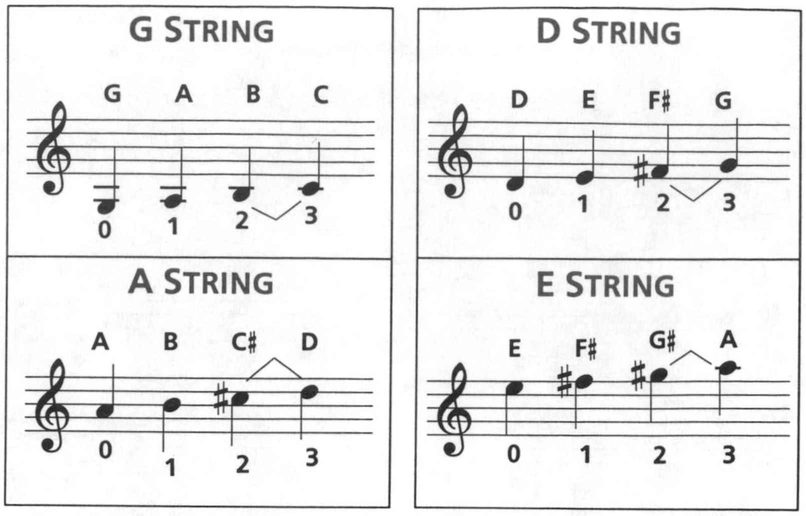

In the major fingering pattern, the distance between the 2nd finger down and the 3rd finger down is a **half step**.
A half step is the smallest interval.
Half steps may be marked:

A half step is also called an interval of a **minor second**.

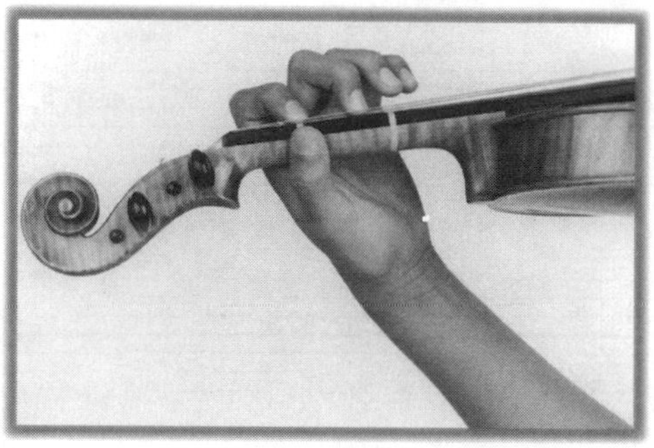

TWO FINGERS DOWN

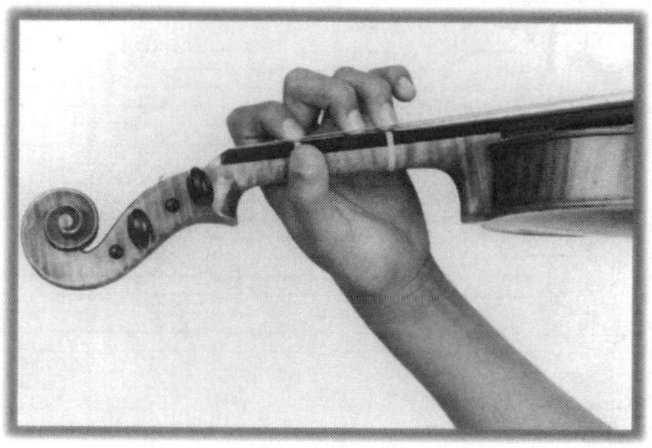

THREE FINGERS DOWN

1. G String Major Fingering Pattern

2. D String Major Fingering Pattern

3. A String Major Fingering Pattern

4. E String Major Fingering Pattern

E String: Violin and Bass only.
C String: Viola and Cello only.

Writing Music

Turn to page 34, line #6. Follow the directions.

MELODIES IN $\frac{3}{4}$ TIME

Time Signature

$\frac{3}{4}$ three beats in a measure; quarter note or quarter rest receives one beat

In $\frac{3}{4}$ time, a whole rest receives three beats of silence.

Dotted Half Note

𝅗𝅥. or 𝅗𝅥.

three beats of sound

1. Rhythm Study

Play on each string.

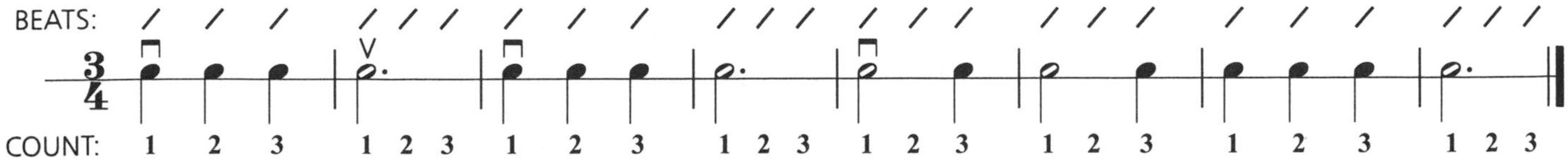

2. Our First Waltz

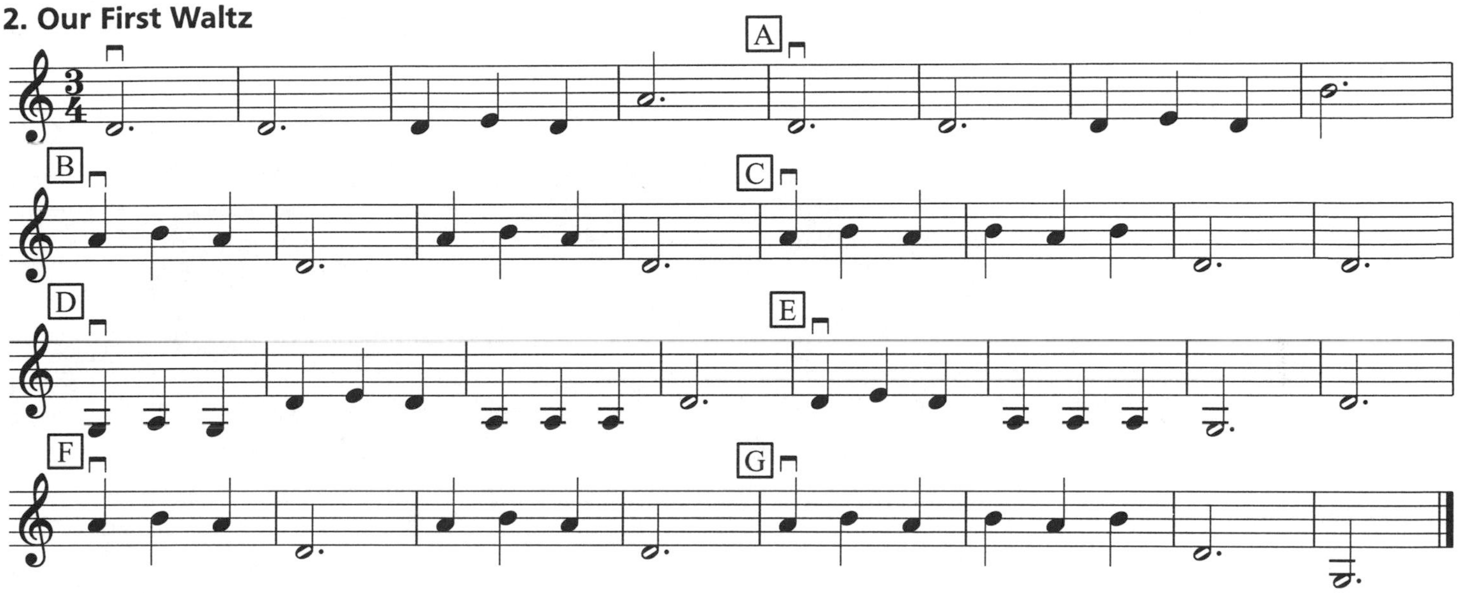

3. Pop Goes the Weasel

Traditional

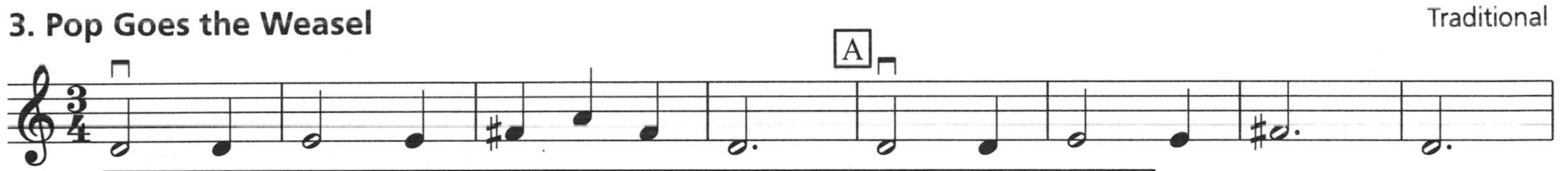

Bowing: For *Half Notes* move the bow slowly. For *Quarter Notes* move the bow quickly.

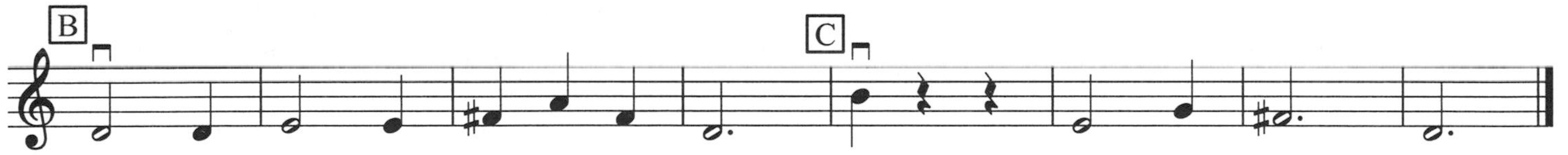

4. Merry-Go-Round

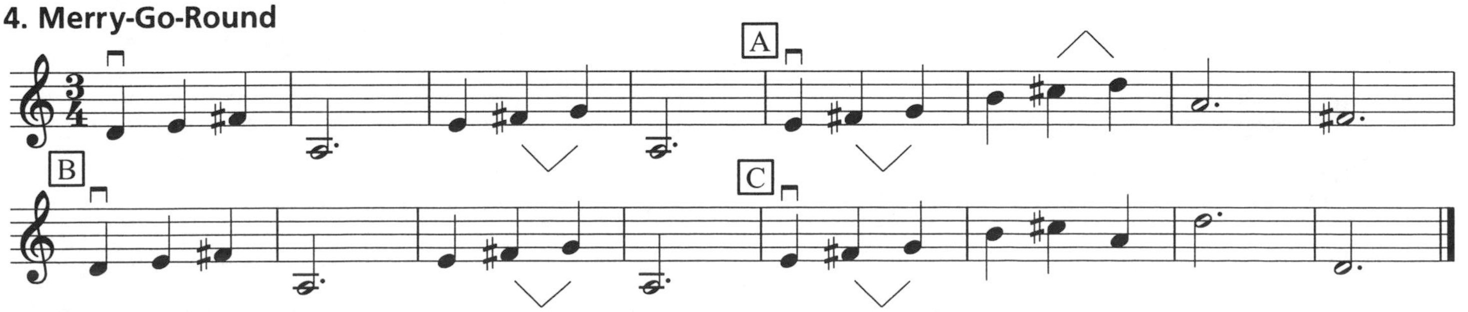

Play *Merry-Go-Round* as written.
Then improvise:

1. Change the rhythm of the 𝅗𝅥. (dotted half notes) to ♩ (quarter notes) and ♫ (two eighth notes).
2. Change the 𝅗𝅥. (dotted half notes) any way you wish.

VII Perfect Intervals

Fourths, **fifths**, and **octaves** are called perfect intervals.
To determine the numerical name of the interval between two notes, count off the lines and spaces from the lower note to the higher note.

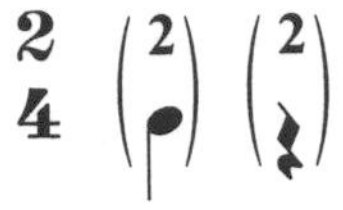

Time Signature
two beats in a measure

quarter note or quarter rest receives one beat
In 2/4 time a whole rest receives two beats of silence.

1. Rhythm Study

Play on each string.

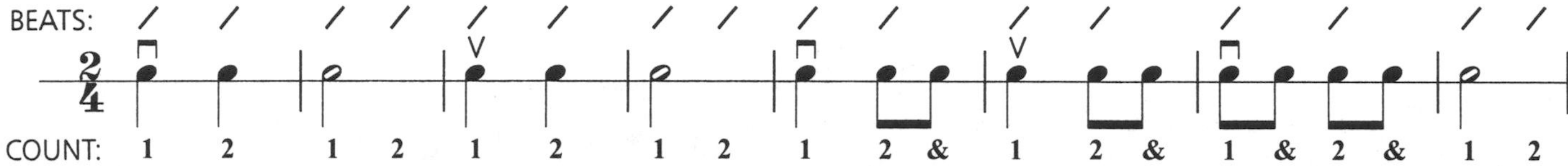

2. Fourths

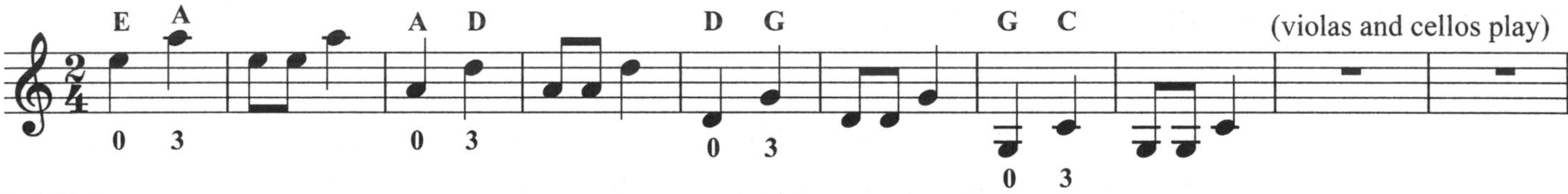

3. Fifths

4. Octaves

FINGERING: 3_________ A line following a fingering means to keep that finger down.

5. Double Stops

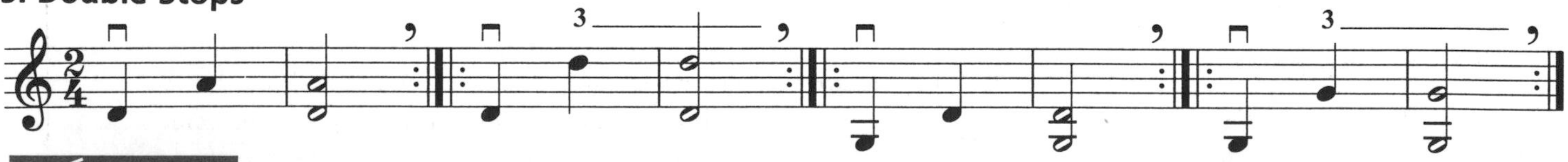

Writing Music

Turn to page 35, line #7. Follow the directions.

Find and name the perfect intervals.

6. Blowing in the Wind

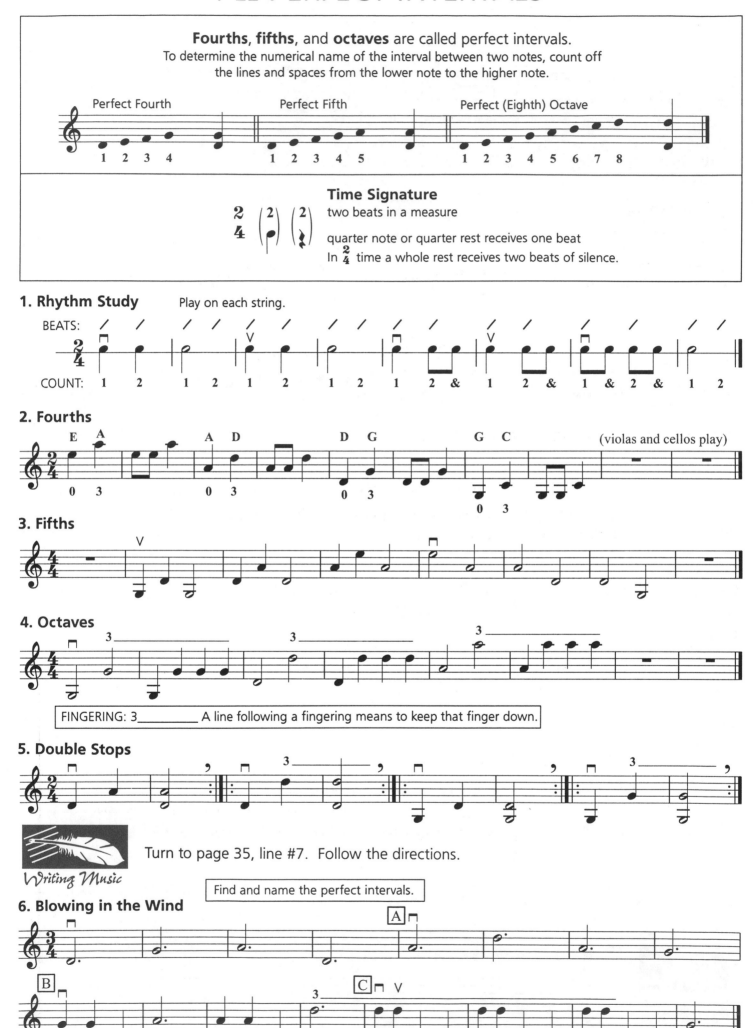

Melodies with Steps and Skips

DYNAMICS	
p = *piano* = soft *f* = *forte* = loud	**Pick-up(s)** - Note(s) played before the first full measure. + - Pluck the string with the left hand finger indicated. **D.C. al Fine** - Go back to the beginning (*Da Capo*) and stop at the end (*Fine*).

1. Old MacDonald

Traditional American

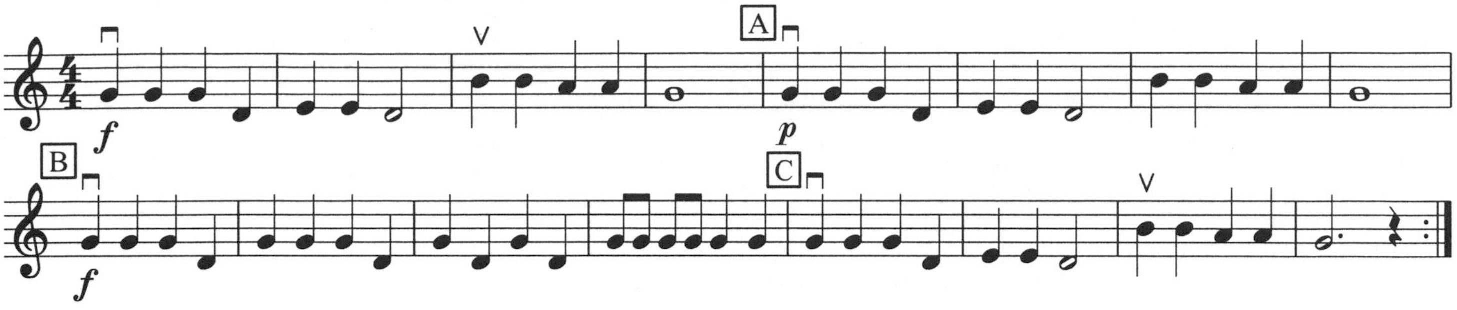

Improvising Music

Play *Old MacDonald* as written.

Then improvise: 1. Change some of the G's to other pitches.

2. Change some of the ♩ (quarter notes) to ♫ (two eighth notes).

2. She'll Be Comin' 'Round the Mountain

Traditional American

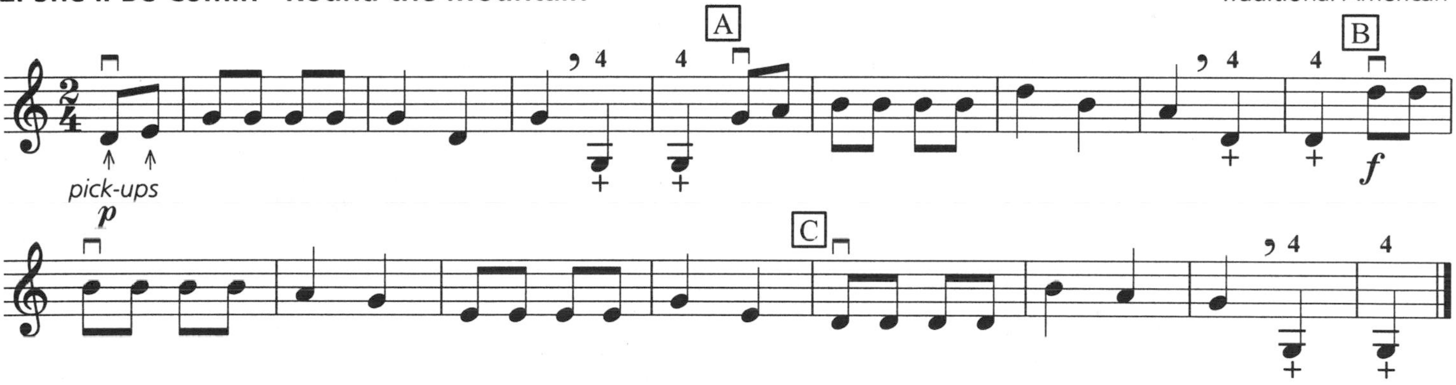

3. Skater's Glide

Find and name the perfect intervals.

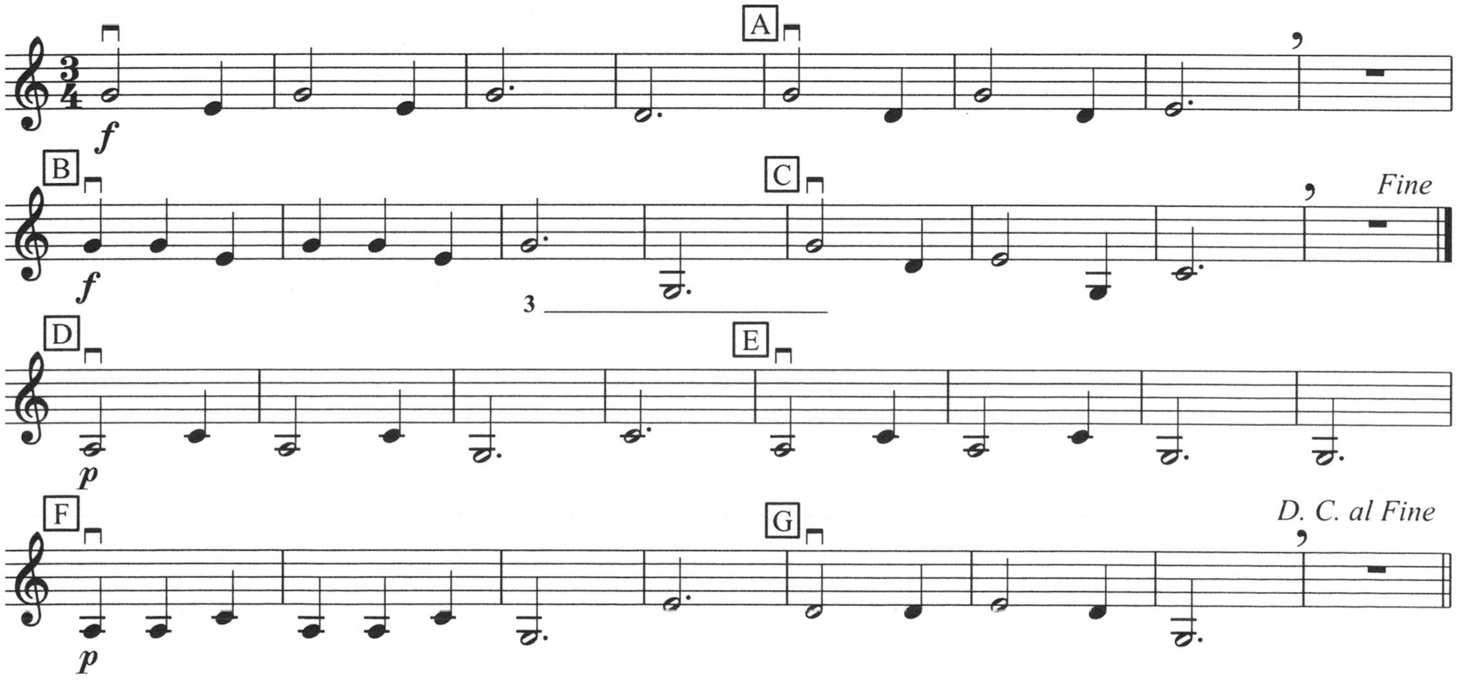

VIII Four Note Minor Fingering Pattern

New Fingering: Whole Step - Half Step - Whole Step

Compare with illustrations on page 14 for the placement of the 2nd finger.

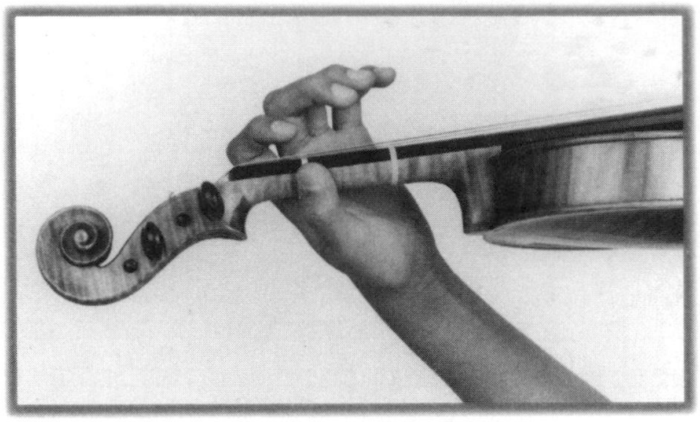

OPEN

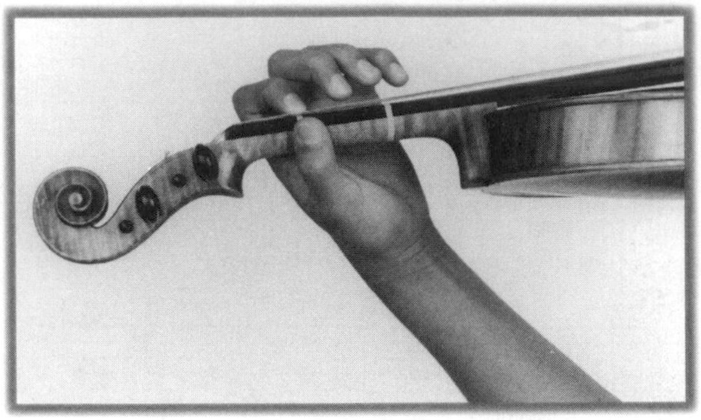

FIRST FINGER DOWN

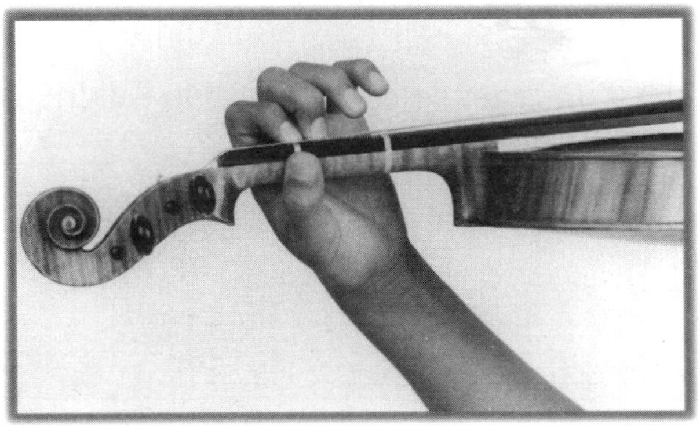

TWO FINGERS DOWN

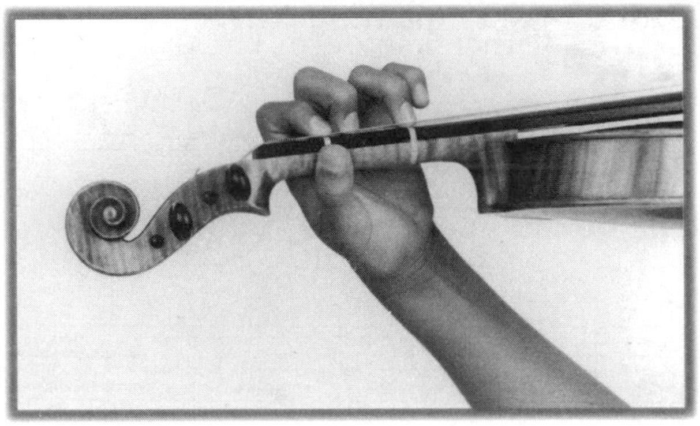

THREE FINGERS DOWN

In the **minor fingering pattern**, the distance between the first finger down and the second finger down is a half step (**minor second**).
The distance between the open string and two fingers down is a whole step plus a half step (**minor third**).

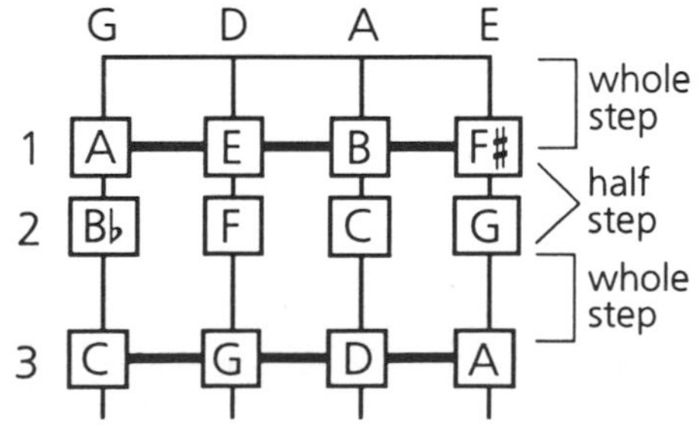

♭ Flat

A **flat** (♭) is a sign that lowers the pitch of a note a half step. The flat sign next to the B changes B to B♭.

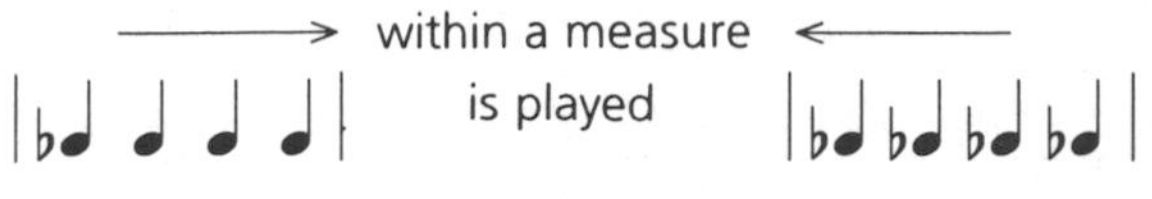

G String

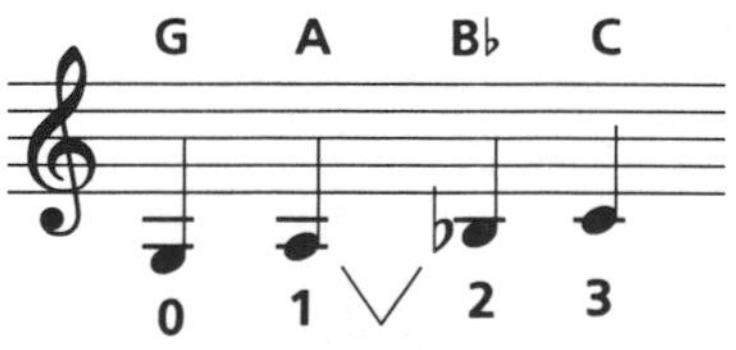

D String

A String

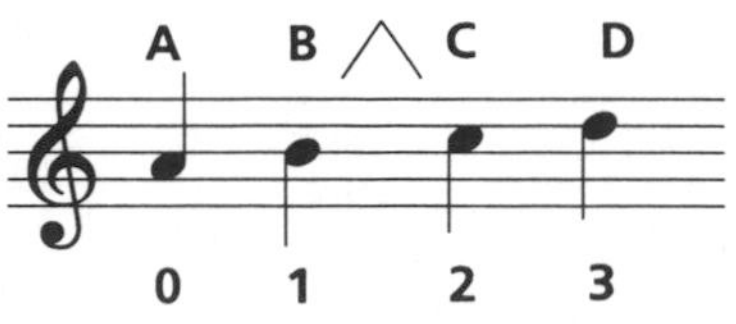

E String

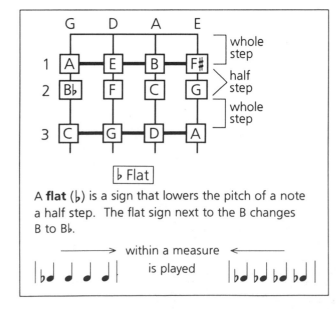

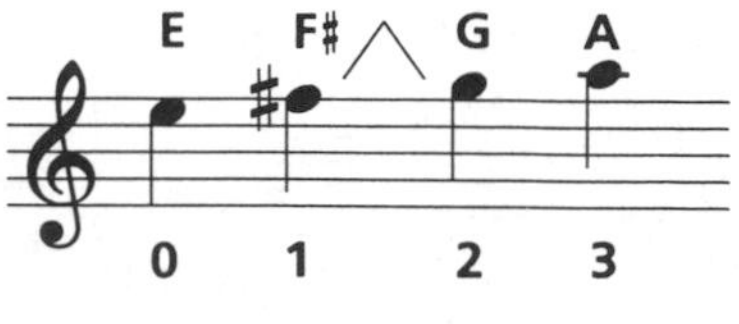

Four Note Minor Fingering Pattern Studies

1. G String Minor Fingering Pattern

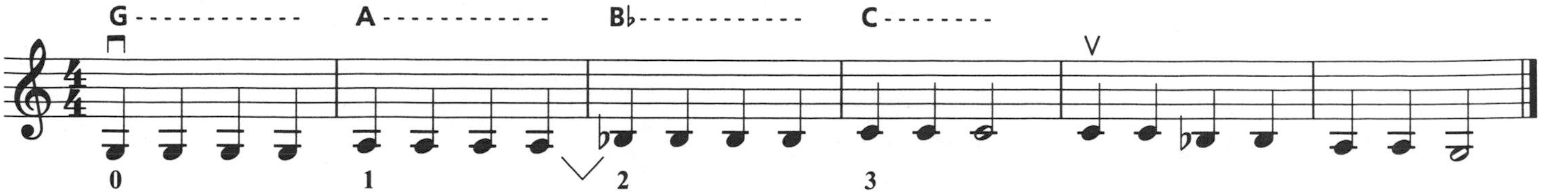

2. D String Minor Fingering Pattern

3. A String Minor Fingering Pattern

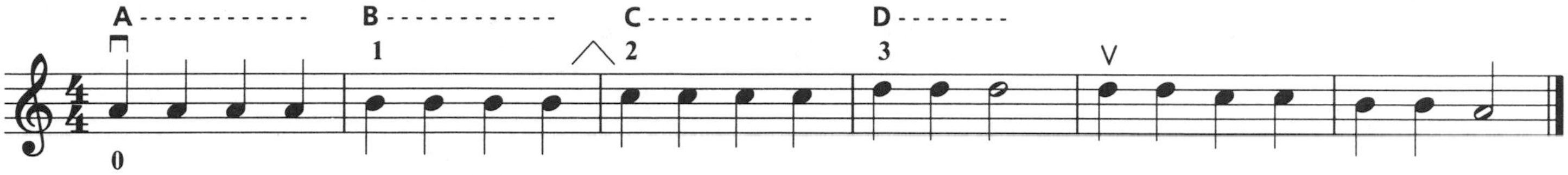

4. E or C String Minor Fingering Pattern

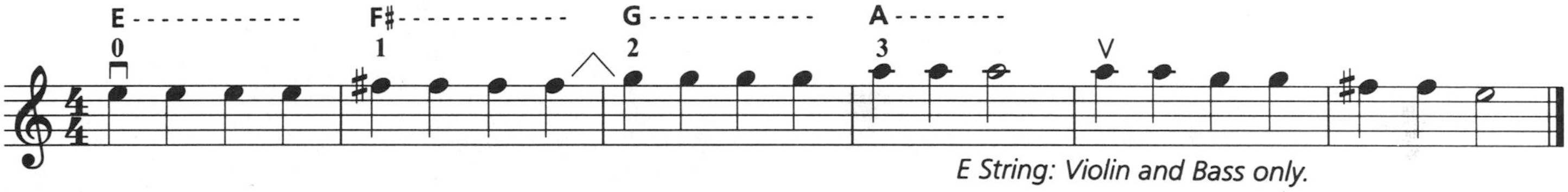

E String: Violin and Bass only.
C String: Viola and Cello only.

5. Open, One, Two

Find and name the whole steps and the half steps.

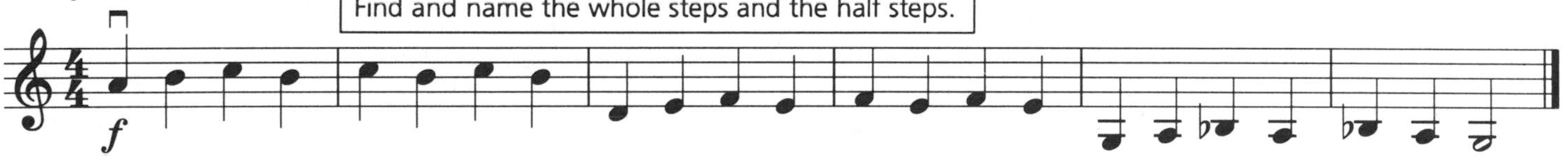

6. Minor Thirds - Up and Down

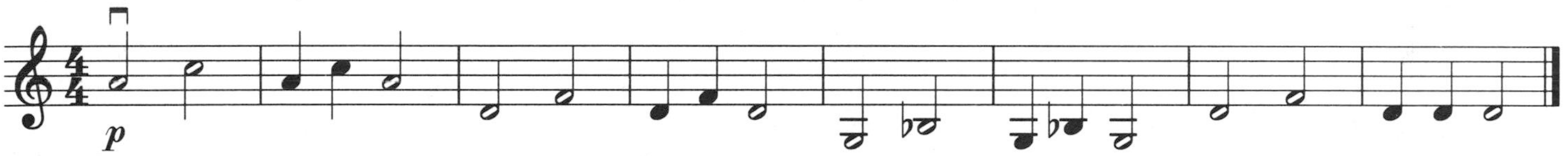

7. Minor March

WB - Whole Bow: Use all of the bow.

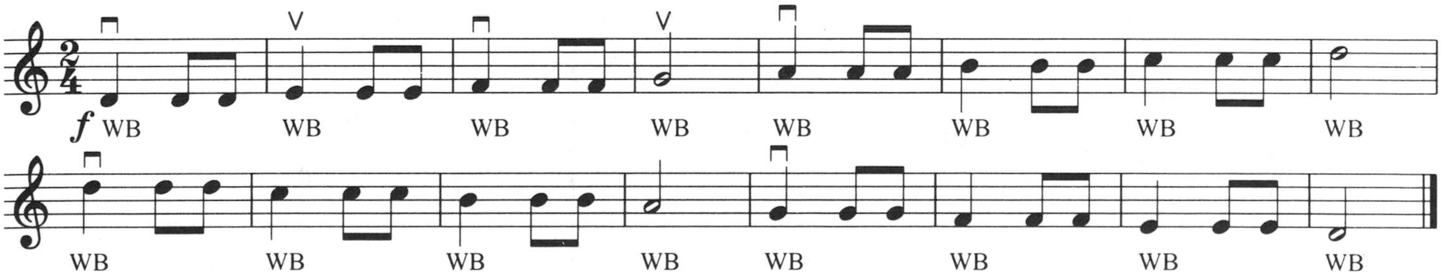

8. Rise Up, O Flame

Michael Praetorius

Play as a canon*.

(4) means optional 4th finger.

*A canon is similar to a round. It is a type of music where musicians play the same melody but enter at different times.

This page may also be played pizzicato.

IX Bowings

Legato and Staccato

LEGATO - The notes sound connected.
Détaché - Broad, alternating bow strokes smoothly connected.
Slur - Two or more notes of different pitch played with one bow stroke.

STACCATO - The notes sound separated and are marked by a dot above or below the notehead.
Martelé - Separated bow strokes. The bow remains **ON** the string.
Spiccato - Separated bow strokes. The bow bounces **OFF** the string. Brush the string with the bow.

Variations on Hot Cross Buns

1. Détaché

English Folk Song

2. Slur

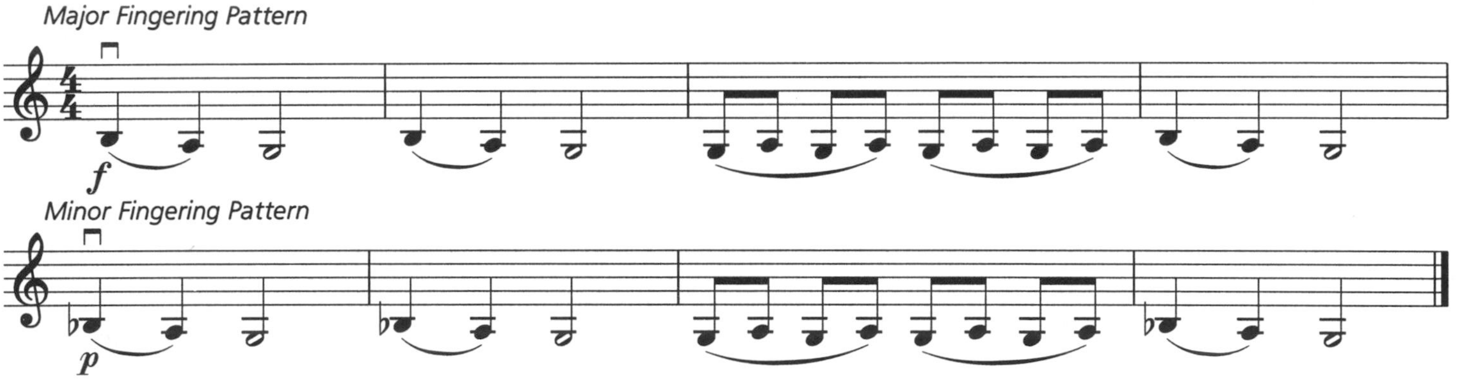

3. Martelé

4. Spiccato

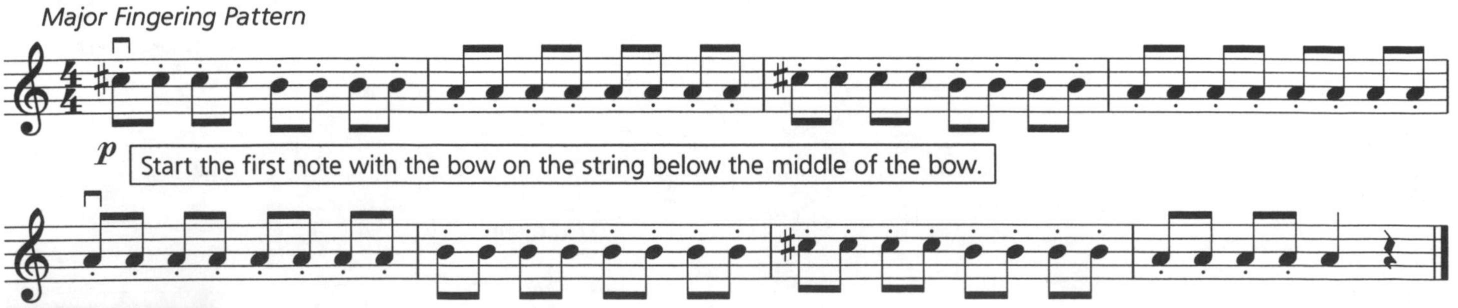

Improvising Music

Improvise your own variation on *Hot Cross Buns*. Try to use at least two of the new bowings.

Melodies with Détaché, Slur, Martelé, and Spiccato Bowings

1. French Folk Song

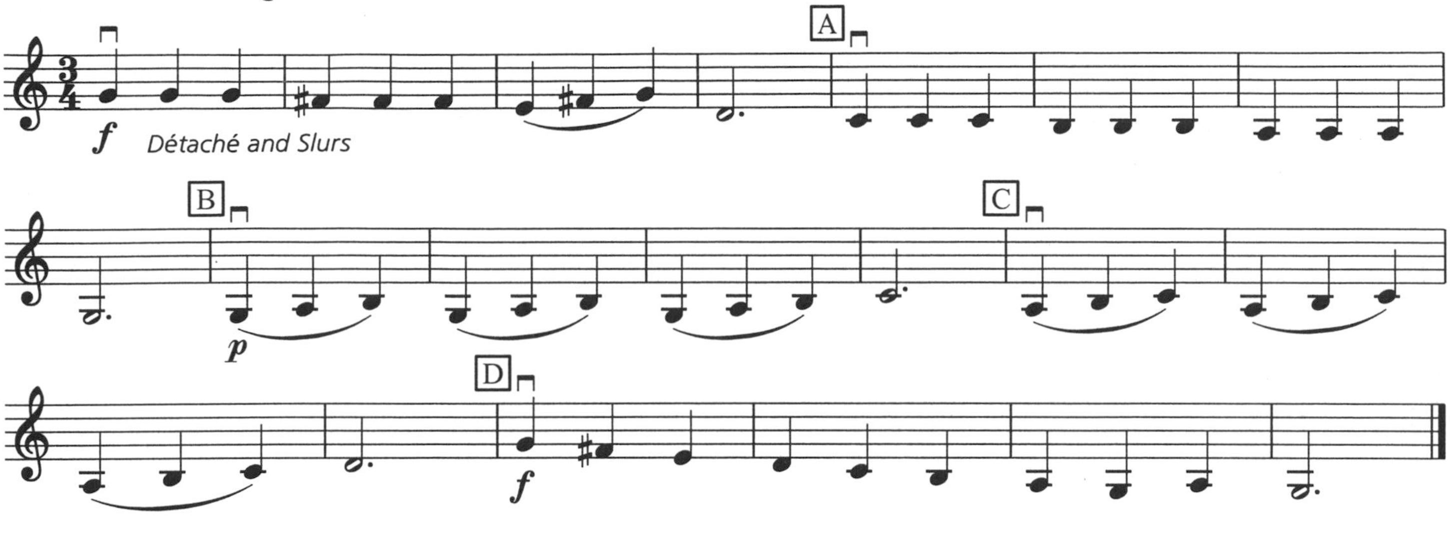

2. If You're Happy

Camp Song

3. My Hat!

German Folk Song

Be sure to play F and C natural.

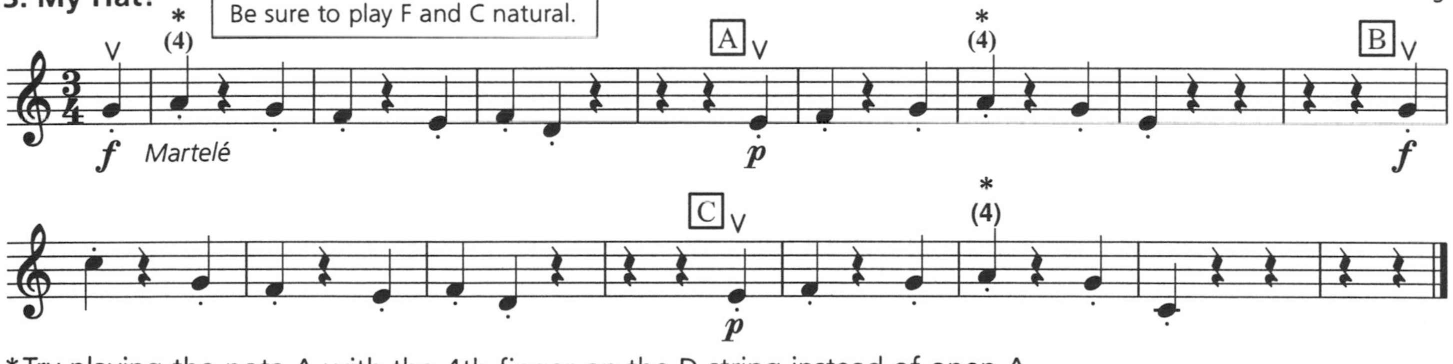

*Try playing the note A with the 4th finger on the D string instead of open A.

4. John Peel

English Folk Song

X The Keys of D Major, C Major, and G Major

A **key** is determined by sharps or flats called a **key signature**. The key signature appears at the beginning of a piece and tells which notes are to be raised or lowered for the entire piece.
A **scale** is a series of notes written or played stepwise in ascending or descending order with a specific sequence of whole steps and half steps determined by the key or key signature.

Key of D Major

In the key of D Major, F and C are sharped in the key signature. Play all F's as F♯ and all C's as C♯. The scale of D Major is in the key of D Major. It begins and ends on D. D is the keynote.

1. D Major Scale

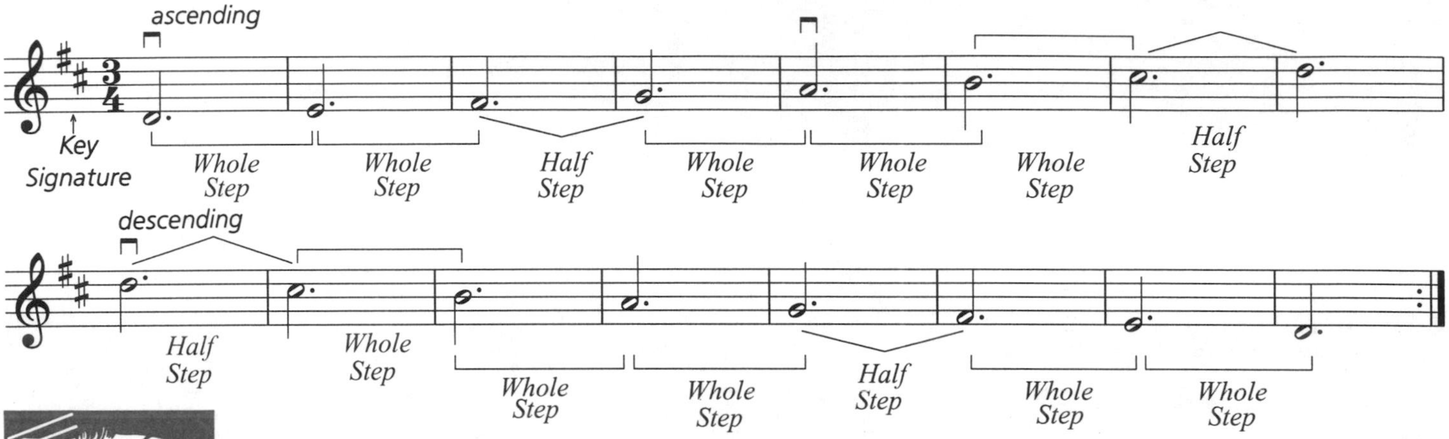

Turn to page 35, line #8. Follow the directions.

2. Variation on the D Major Scale

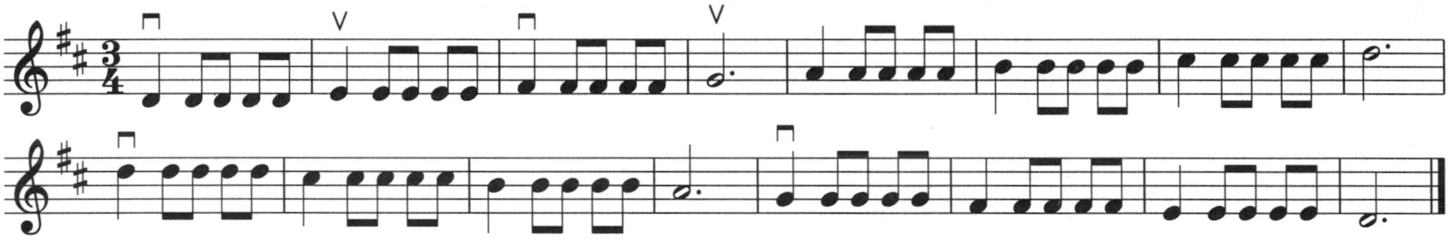

3. Violin Concerto Theme

Ludwig van Beethoven

FINGERING: ③ A fingering in a circle means place only that finger on the string.

4. Gavotte

George Frederick Handel

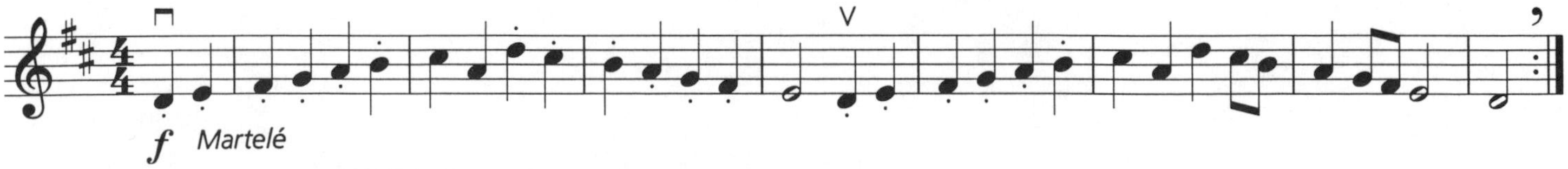

5. Hang Gliding

1st time - *arco*, 2nd time - *pizz.*

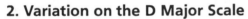

Tie - A curved line connecting two notes of the same pitch.

Slur - A curved line indicating two or more notes of different pitches played with one bow stroke.

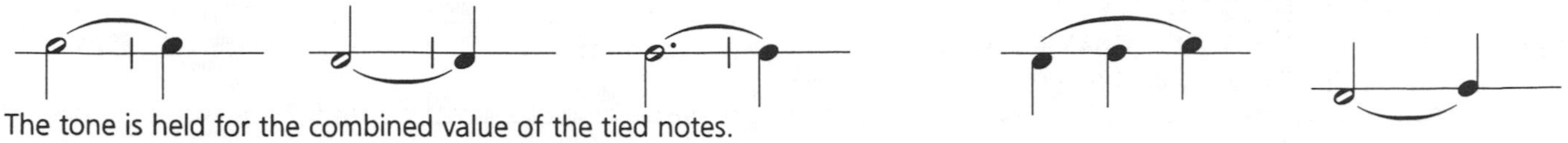

The tone is held for the combined value of the tied notes.

Play *Hang Gliding* as written

Then Improvise:
1. by changing some of the ♩ (quarter notes) to ♫ (two eighth notes).
2. by changing the pitch of the notes on the 2nd and 3rd beats.
3. by changing and adding notes any way you like.

6. Row, Row, Row Your Boat *Play as a round.*

Traditional Round

7. Interval of the Third

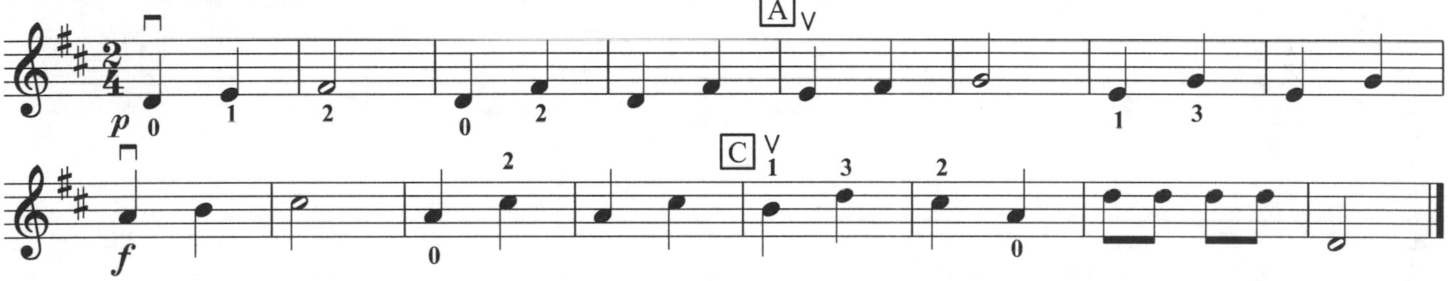

8. Andale Juana

Mexican Folk Song

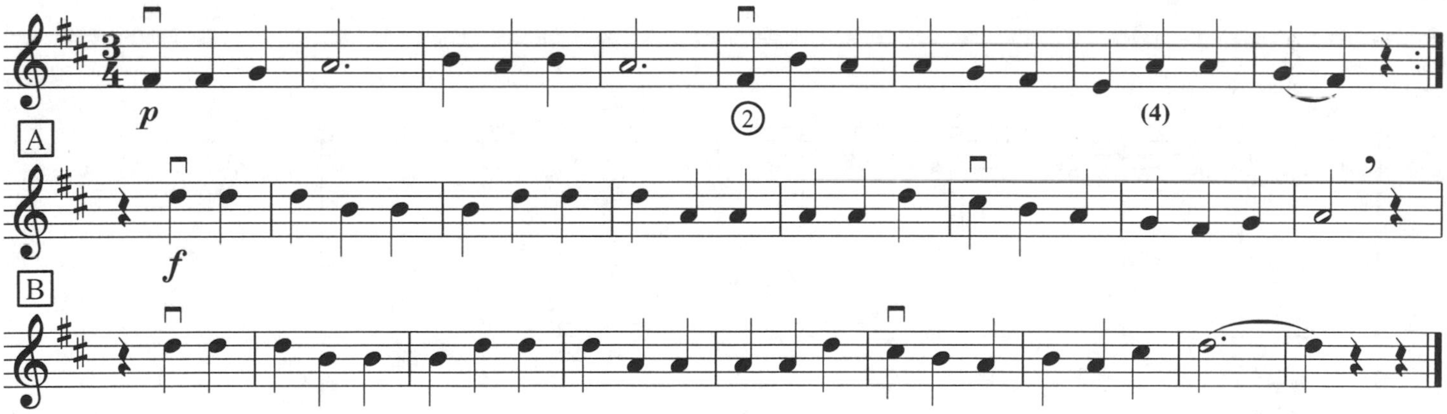

9. Bugle Call

Traditional

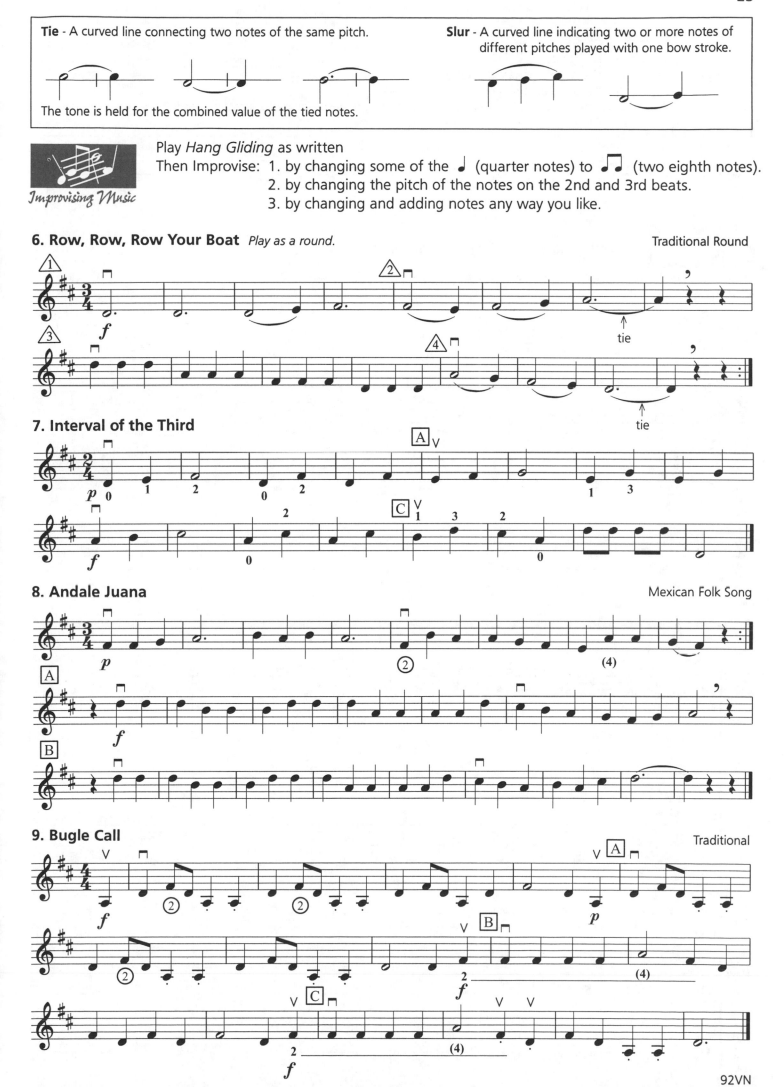

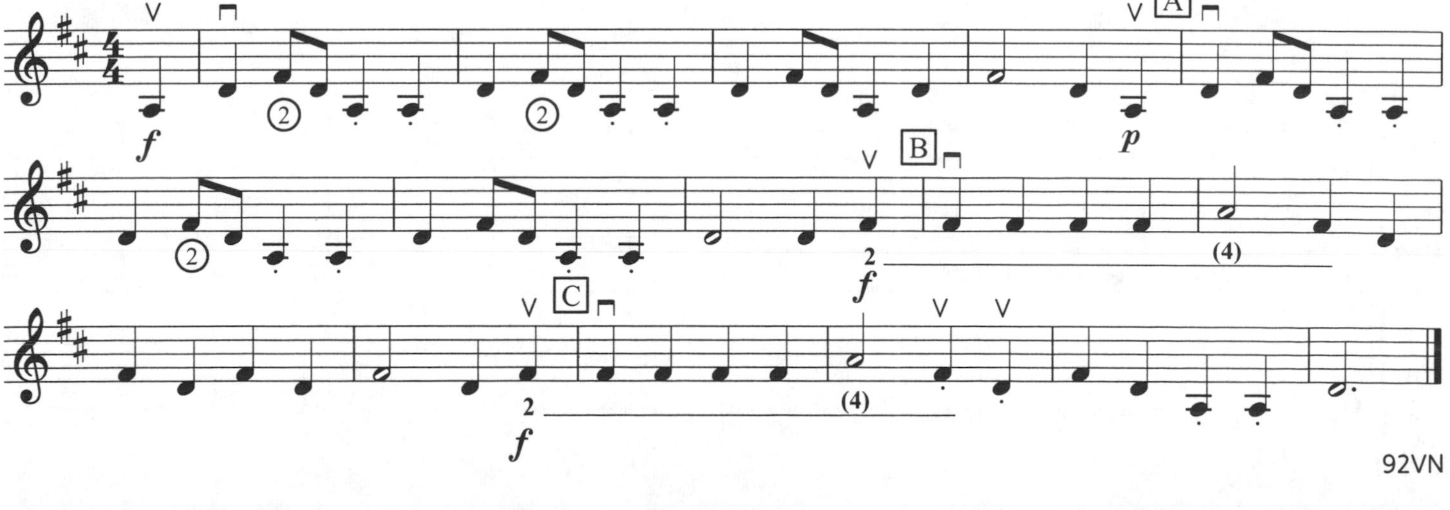

KEY OF C MAJOR

In the key of **C Major**, there are no sharps in the key signature.
The scale of C Major is in the key of C Major. It begins and ends on C. C is the keynote.

1. C Major Scale

Writing Music

Turn to page 35, line #9. Follow the directions.

2. Folk Song

German Folk Song

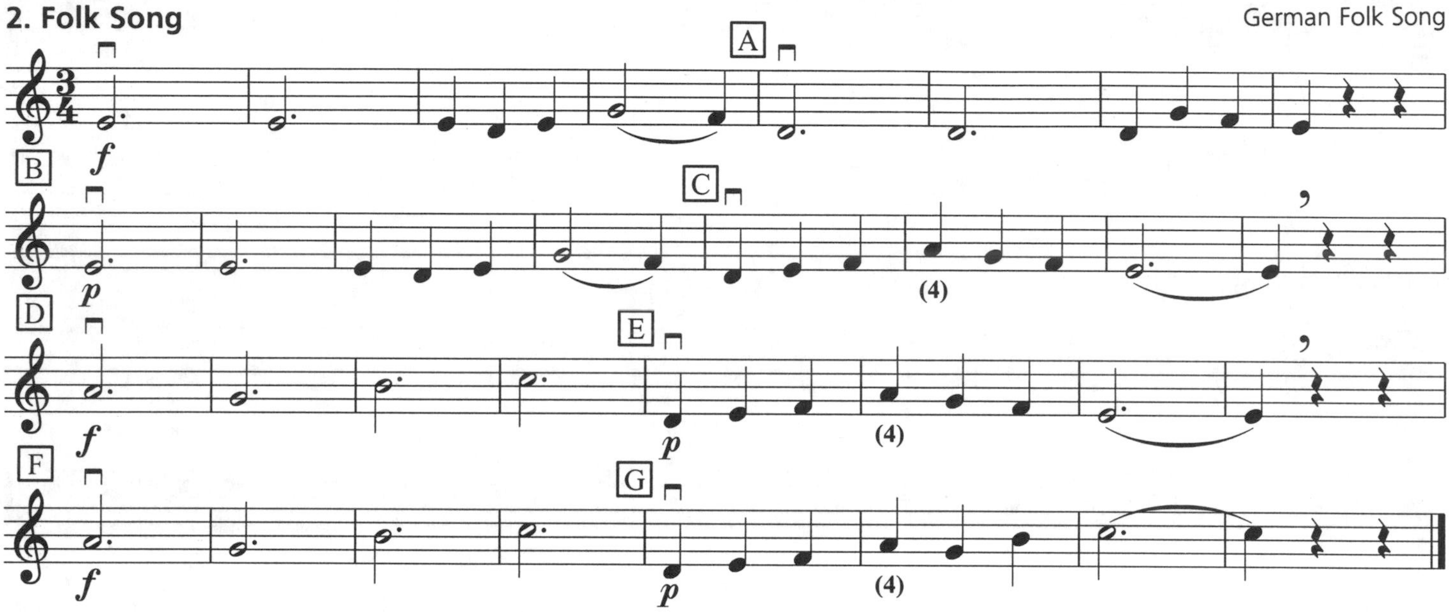

3. Jacob's Ladder - Trio

BOWING: For quarter notes move the bow quickly. For dotted half notes move the bow slowly.

American Spiritual

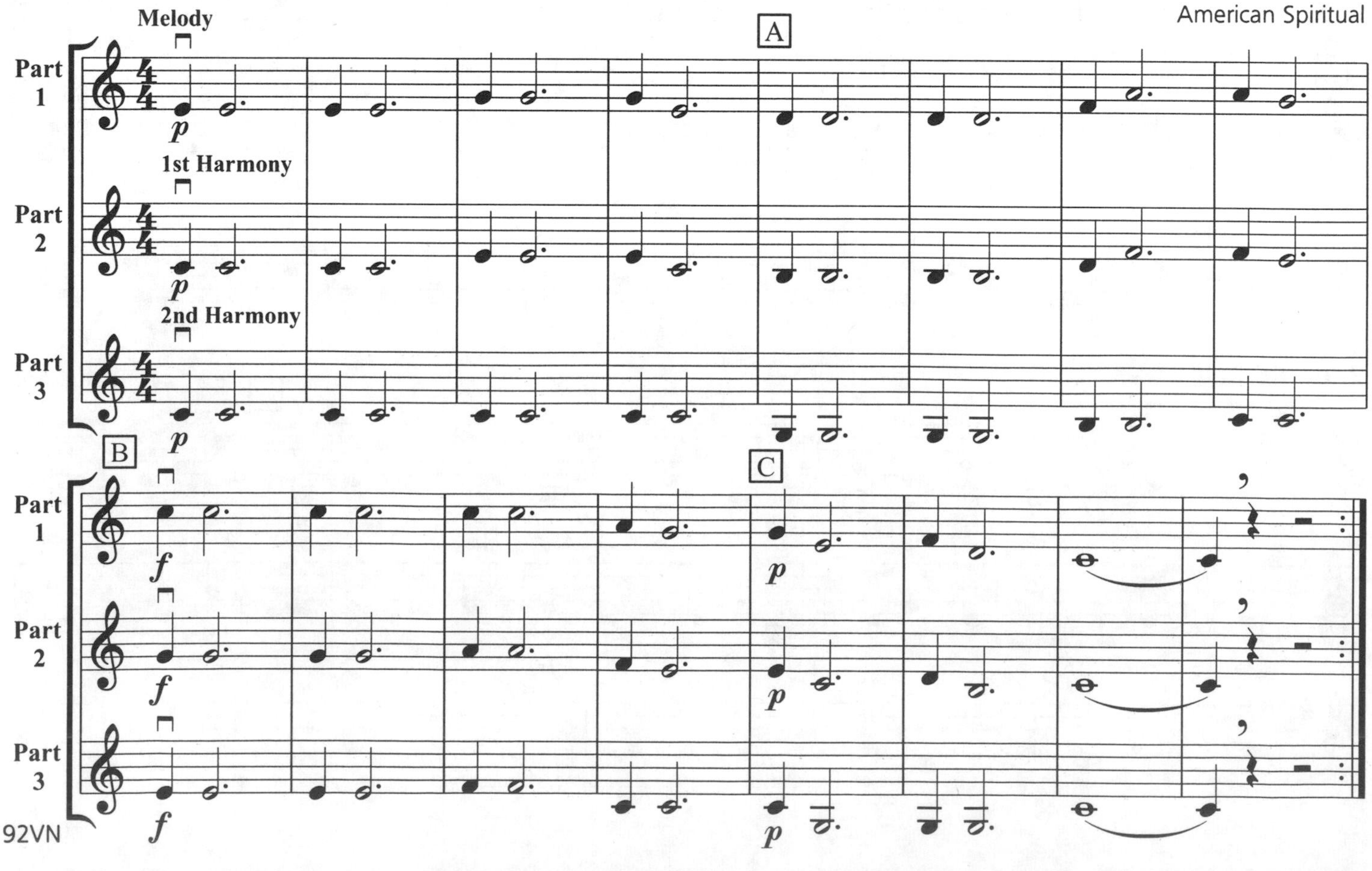

4. Country Gardens

Détaché, Slurs, and Martelé

Old English Dance

* *f-p* means play loudly the 1st time. Play softly on the repeat.

5. Tinga Layo

Jamaican Folk Song

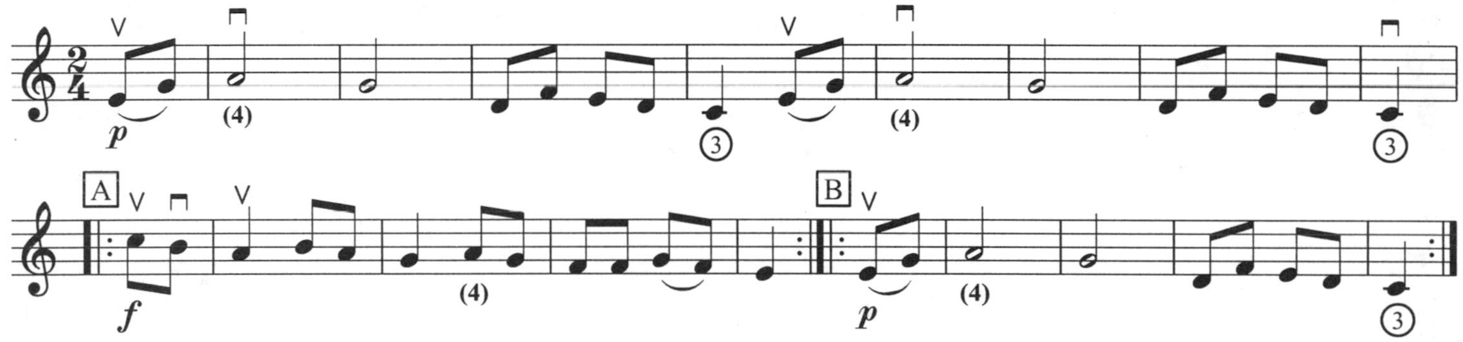

6. Alphabet Song - Duet

Lively!

Learn to sing the Alphabet Song.

Wolfgang Amadeus Mozart

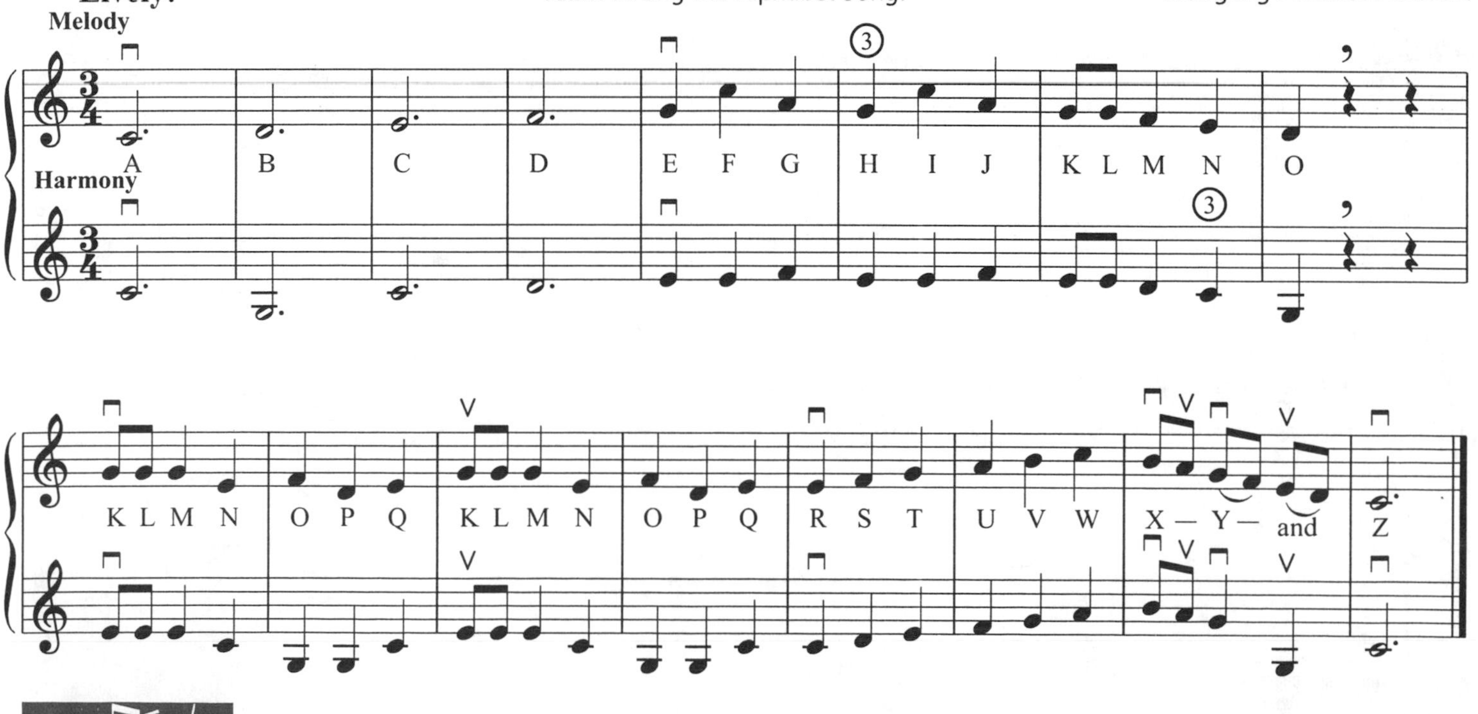

Improvising Music

Improvise on the first four (dotted half) notes in the melody part of the *Alphabet Song*.

KEY OF G MAJOR

In the key of **G Major**, F is sharped in the key signature. Play all F's as F♯. The scale of G Major is in the key of G Major. It begins and ends on G. G is the keynote.

1. G Major Scale

2. Michael Finnegan

Traditional

On the last note, lift the bow with a flourish!

3. Strutter's March

Writing Music

Turn to page 35, line #10. Follow the directions.

4. Dance of the Happy Spirits

Christoph Gluck

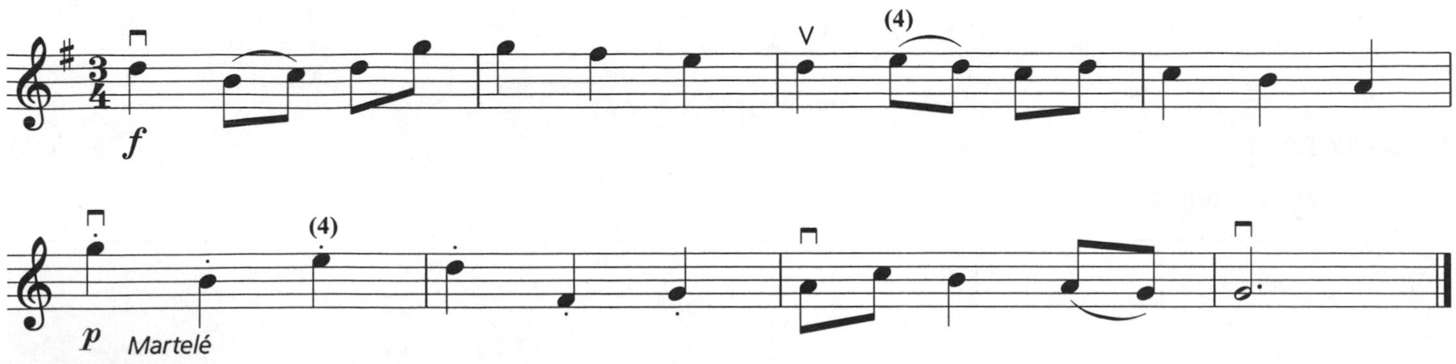

Improvising Music

Improvise your own new melody in the key of G Major.
Begin and end your melody on G.

5. White Coral Bells

Traditional Round

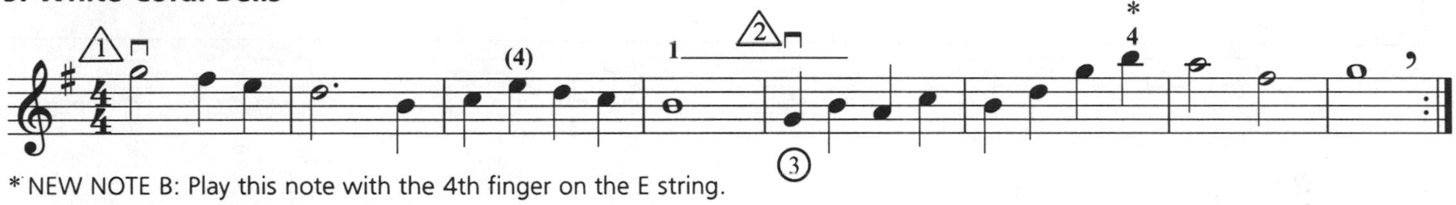

* NEW NOTE B: Play this note with the 4th finger on the E string.

6. Madalina Catalina

Camp Song

* *sfz* – Play with a sudden strong accent.

XI Harmonized Melodies

Star Song

Three Part Harmony*

MELODY PART

Traditional

ENSEMBLE PART

*Each section may divide with half playing the melody part and half playing the ensemble part.

Jingle Bells

Three Part Harmony*

MELODY PART

J. S. Pierpont

ENSEMBLE PART

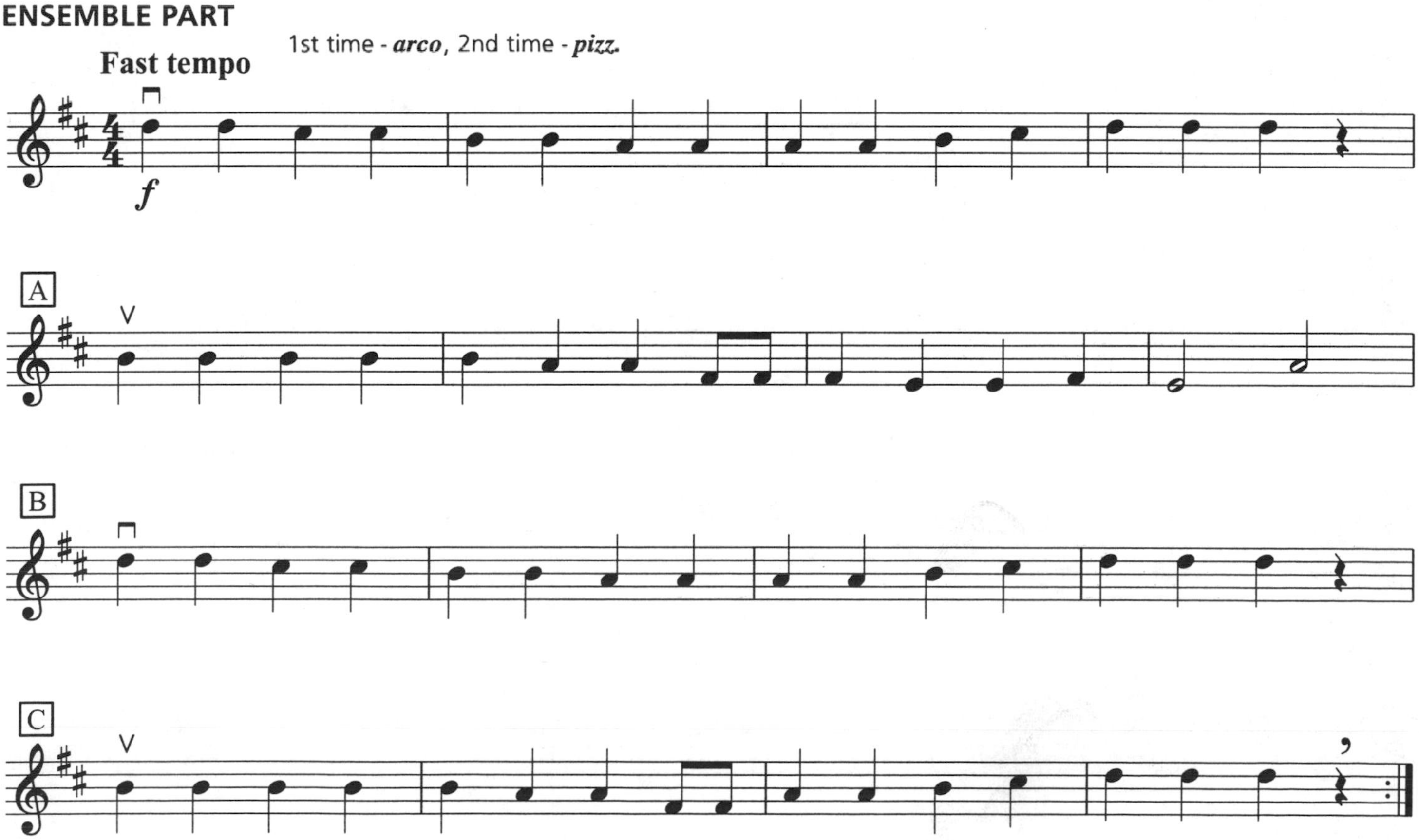

*Each section may divide with half playing the melody part and half playing the ensemble part.

Simple Gifts

Three Part Harmony*

Shaker Melody

MELODY PART

ENSEMBLE PART

*Each section may divide with half playing the melody part and half playing the ensemble part.

Lightly Row

Three Part Harmony*

MELODY PART

Traditional

ENSEMBLE PART

*Each section may divide with half playing the melody part and half playing the ensemble part.

CHOPSTICKS

Three Part Harmony*

MELODY PART

Fast tempo

Traditional

*Each section may divide with half playing the melody part and half playing the ensemble part.

(*Chopsticks*, continued)

ENSEMBLE PART

Fast tempo

Traditional

XII WRITING MUSIC

1. Copy each music symbol in the space next to it.

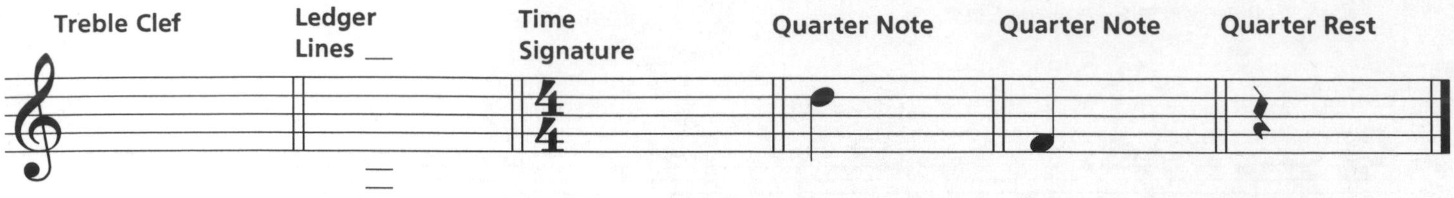

2. Copy this music _ _ _ _ _ _ _ _ _ _ _ _ _ _ _ _ _ here, exactly as you see it. Play the music.

3. Copy this music _ _ _ _ _ _ _ _ _ _ _ _ _ _ _ _ _ here, exactly as you see it. Play the music.

4. Write your clef sign and $\frac{4}{4}$ time signature. Write two measures of music for your highest open string and two measures for your lowest open string. Use quarter notes and half notes. Play the music that you write.

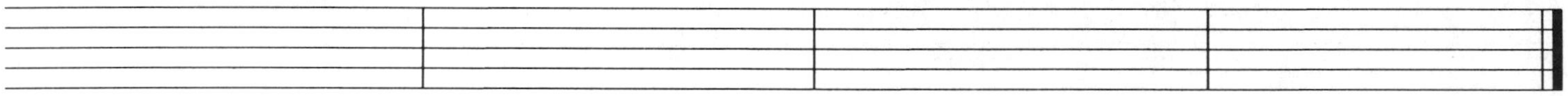

5. Write your clef sign and the $\frac{4}{4}$ time signature. Write four measures of music for your two middle strings. Use quarter notes and half notes. Play the music that you write.

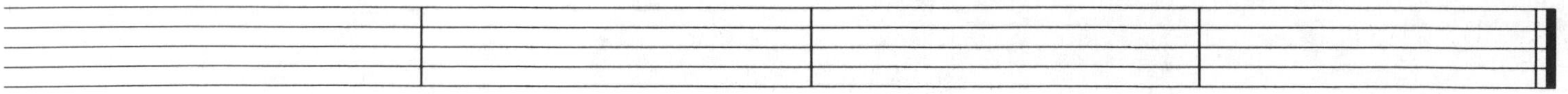

6. Write a six measure melody on one string in $\frac{4}{4}$ time. Use quarter notes, half notes, and eighth notes. Begin and end your piece on the open string. Play your melody as written and play it on the other strings.

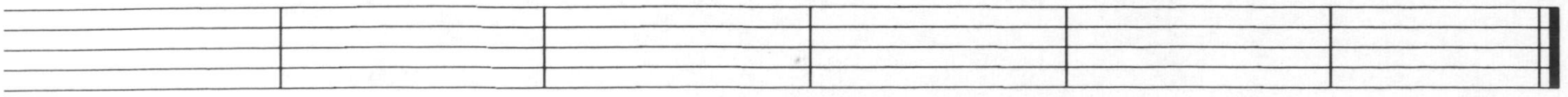

7. Write a six measure melody in your clef in $\frac{4}{4}$ time. Write music to be played on two strings. Play your melody and then improvise on it.

8. Write the D Major Scale in quarter notes.
Name each note.

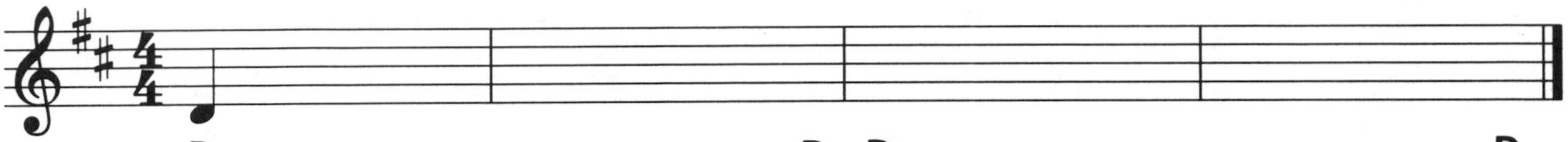

D __ __ __ __ __ __ D D __ __ __ __ __ __ D

9. Write the C Major Scale in half notes. The key signature has no sharps or flats.
Name each note.

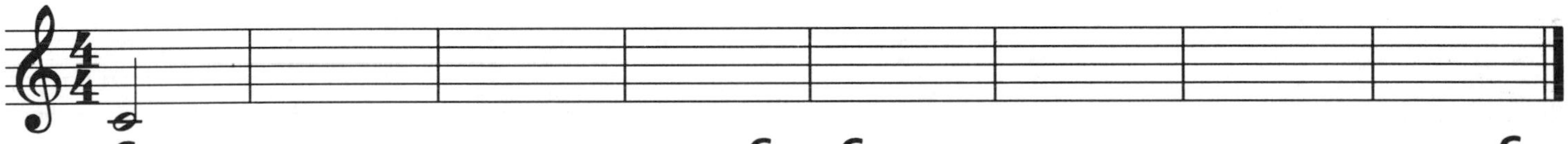

C __ __ __ __ __ __ C C __ __ __ __ __ __ C

10. Write an eight measure melody in the key of G Major. The key signature of G Major is one sharp.
Begin and end your melody on G. Use either the $\frac{3}{4}$ or $\frac{2}{4}$ time signature.
Play your melody and then improvise on it.

Now you are ready to write more music. You will need a music manuscript book for your new compositions.
Try to make your manuscript neat and easy to read. Think of a new, short tune.
Try playing it on your instrument. Then try to write it in your manuscript book.
If it doesn't come out exactly the way you'd like, just turn the page and start over again.
Writing music is exciting and lots of fun. **GOOD LUCK!**

Try Writing Your Own Compositions Here!